BAILOUTS

The Columbia University Press and Social Science Research Council
Series on the Privatization of Risk

THE COLUMBIA UNIVERSITY PRESS AND SOCIAL SCIENCE RESEARCH COUNCIL SERIES ON THE PRIVATIZATION OF RISK

Edited by Craig Calhoun and Jacob S. Hacker

The early twenty-first century is witnessing a concerted effort to privatize risk—to shift responsibility for the management or mitigation of key risks onto private-sector organizations or directly onto individuals. This series uses social science research to analyze this issue in depth. Each volume presents a concise review of a particular topic from the perspective of the public and private allocation of risk and responsibility and offers analysis and empirical, evidence-based opinion from leading scholars in the fields of economics, political science, sociology, anthropology, and law. Support for the series comes from the John D. and Catherine T. MacArthur Foundation.

Jacob S. Hacker, ed., *Health at Risk: America's Ailing Health System—and How to Heal It*

Andrew Lakoff, ed., *Disaster and the Politics of Intervention*

Donald W. Light, ed., *The Risks of Prescription Drugs*

Katherine S. Newman, ed., *Laid Off, Laid Low: Political and Economic Consequences of Employment Insecurity*

Mitchell A. Orenstein, ed., *Pensions, Social Security, and the Privatization of Risk*

Bailouts: Public Money, Private Profit

EDITED BY ROBERT E. WRIGHT

COLUMBIA UNIVERSITY PRESS | NEW YORK

A COLUMBIA/SSRC BOOK

COLUMBIA UNIVERSITY PRESS
Publishers Since 1893
New York   Chichester, West Sussex

Copyright © 2010 The Social Science Research Council
All rights reserved

Library of Congress Cataloging-in-Publication Data

Bailouts : public money, private profit / Robert E. Wright,
editor.
    p.   cm.—(The Columbia University Press
and Social Science Research Council series on the
privatization of risk)
    Includes bibliographical references.
    ISBN 978-0-231-15054-5 (cloth : alk. paper)—
ISBN 978-0-231-15055-2 (pbk. : alk. paper)—
ISBN 978-0-231-52173-4 (ebook)
        1. Financial crises—United States. 2. Finance—
Government policy—United States. 3. Bank failures—
United States. 4. Intervention (Federal government)—
United States. 5. Corporate reorganizations—
United States. 6. Corporate turnarounds—United
States. I. Wright, Robert E. (Robert Eric), 1969–
II. Title. III. Series.

HB3722.B35 2009
338.973'02—dc22

2009031806

Columbia University Press books are printed
on permanent and durable acid-free paper. This
book is printed on paper with recycled content.
Printed in the United States of America

c 10 9 8 7 6 5 4 3 2 1
p 10 9 8 7 6 5 4 3 2 1

References to Internet Web sites (URLs) were
accurate at the time of writing. Neither the editor
nor Columbia University Press is responsible
for URLs that may have expired or changed since
the manuscript was prepared.

Design by Julie Fry
Cover by Vin Dang

CONTENTS

BAILOUTS

To Bail or Not to Bail?

ROBERT E. WRIGHT

The verb "to bail out" means to implement a bailout. The noun "bail-out," in this volume and I believe more generally, refers to instances when the government aids one or more economically distressed businesses in some way. Big picture, bailouts are simply one of many forms of government interaction with the economy and the producers and consumers that inhabit it. Governments proscribe certain activities — or at least attempt to. For example, they try to ban the production, sale, or use of certain chemicals, like LSD and crystal meth. They sometimes try merely to discourage consumption of certain goods, like gasoline, by taxing them or otherwise raising their cost, for instance by restricting the places where tobacco can be lawfully smoked. Governments also try to encourage certain behaviors through tax incentives and sundry sorts of subsidies. In the United States, for example, the Department of Defense directly aided over 3,600 defense contractors between 1958 and 1973, and since the Depression, the Department of Agriculture has plied farmers with billions of dollars in cash aid and subsidized loans. Almost invariably, governments claim to interact with the economy to improve it in some way. Often, however, government officials implement policies at least partially designed to fatten their own wallets or, in less corrupt nations, to enhance their electoral prospects by bestowing favors upon influential groups, like labor unions and major corporations.[1]

Governments also try to manage macroeconomic outcomes, including per capita output and unemployment, exchange, interest, and inflation rates. Whenever an unexpected shock, like a natural catastrophe, terrorist attack, or financial crisis, threatens economic growth or employment levels, the affected government comes under pressure, domestic and international, to respond. Often, governments try to bail out distressed firms in the hope of maintaining employment and output. Bailouts seem like common sense until we realize that they are costly and may not produce the desired effect. Some, perhaps most, bailouts initiated in response to financial crises redistribute resources, often from the innocent and poor to the blameworthy rich, without speeding the return to economic prosperity and are actually planting the seeds of the next crisis. Yet the failure to bail out could cause a protracted economic downturn that would hurt everyone, but most especially the poor, aged, unskilled, and otherwise vulnerable.

To bail or not to bail is the Shakespearian question that confronts Americans today, and it does not admit of an easy answer. On the one hand, people fear that if the government does not respond to the financial crisis with vigor, another Great Depression may bring back bread lines; desperately squalid mothers pining for the well-being of their dirty, shack-dwelling children; and Rose of Sharon Joad suckling a starving man in a barn with the breast milk nature intended for her stillborn child.[2] Route 66 may again be cluttered with old cars, only this time the exodus will be *from* a parched and over-farmed California, not to it.[3] On the other hand, Americans also fear that bailouts unfairly reward risky behavior; take money out of their pockets for the benefit of the rich, the dumb, and the greedy; and may not get the economy growing again. A few even suspect that bailouts can turn a recession into a depression by interfering with normal market mechanisms.

Americans' fears are well justified. Government inaction could allow a bad situation to get worse, but so too could an overzealous government reaction. Narratives of the Great Depression make both claims. Some bash Herbert Hoover for sitting on his hands, while others blame government interference, including the Smoot-Hawley tariff, a bumbling Federal Reserve, and disruptive New Deal policies, for transforming a natural downturn into an international calamity.[4]

Both stories are in some sense right. The key to vitiating any systemic crisis, as the contributors to this volume see it, is for government to implement just the right type of bailout. Discerning what policy or policies that entails, however, is far from clear. Theory is of limited use here, we believe. What ultimately matters is reality, which prompts us to ask empirical questions like: What are financial crises and what causes them? What is a bailout? What types of bailouts have been tried? When, where, and why? Did they aid the economy and by what measure? If so, why? If not, why not? What unintended consequences or side effects can bailouts cause?

The authors of the chapters in this volume address those questions through the lenses of history and statistics. They do not always agree on the details, but their conclusions point in the same direction. Different types or degrees of crises demand different types of bailouts. Context is crucial. In the late 1980s and early 1990s, for example, the creation of a so-called bad bank, the Resolution Trust Corporation, worked fairly well to resolve a crisis of insolvent savings and loans. The same approach, however, may not work to end the current crisis, which has struck a relatively few large, complex financial institutions and not, as in the 1980s, hundreds of smallish depository institutions.

If carefully chosen and implemented, bailouts can slow or even stop further economic deterioration by restoring order to markets and confidence to businesses and investors. There is no statistical evidence, however, that bailouts can speed economic recovery. In fact, bailouts can slow recovery by creating policy uncertainty, distorting market incentives, and in extreme cases fomenting sociopolitical unrest. Contrary to common perception, the U.S. government does not bail out every distressed industry that asks it for aid. To date, its bailouts have been directed toward the financial system, the proper functioning of which most experts agree is crucial to economic stability, large industries like railroads and automobile manufacturing, and broad segments of the population, including taxpayers and homeowners. Nevertheless, the redistributive aspects of bailouts continue to cause considerable consternation for citizens and lawmakers.

It is the redistributive qualities of bailouts that I focus on in the first chapter, "Hybrid Failures and Bailouts: Social Costs, Private Profits." Hyper-dysfunctional parts of the economy, including financial crises, are rooted in hybrid failures, or complex combinations of both market failures, like asymmetric information, externalities, public goods, and asset bubbles, and government failures, like inadequate or inappropriate regulation and distortions caused by the tax system and social engineering. In that sense, crises are caused by complex societal forces, and hence a social response to them is both warranted and justified. On the other hand, some types of bailouts are clearly unjustified because they enable private concerns (individuals, corporations, entire industries) to take one-sided bets where they earn private profits when conditions are good but impose losses on society when conditions are bad. That arrangement exacerbates moral hazard or unjustified risk taking, which in turn increases the likelihood and severity of crises. Taking resources from taxpayers to help stoke the fires of crisis is clearly not good policy.

What, then, to do? As a historian, I suggest that a policy akin to Hamilton's Rule (formerly Bagehot's Rule) would serve best. Treasury secretary Alexander Hamilton, like Walter Bagehot and other central banking theorists after him, showed during the Panic of 1792 that the government can thwart a financial panic by lending at a penalty rate to all borrowers who can post good collateral. The collateral requirement ensures that only safe firms receive aid. The penalty rate ensures that firms borrow from the government only as a last resort. The economic pain of borrowing at a high rate, even if it is just a percentage point or two above the usual level, limits moral hazard and risk taking. The rule also minimizes losses to taxpayers by requiring that loans be well collateralized and yield a good return. In fact, the government (and hence ultimately taxpayers) may actually profit from such policy implementation.

Some economists believe that Hamilton's Rule can be applied effectively internationally as well.[5] That is an important consideration today due to globalization and the increasingly multinational scope of the world's largest and most important financial and manufacturing enterprises. Historically, increased interconnectedness is associated with financial crises more global in nature because troubles in one country spread more easily to others.[6] The Japanese banking crisis of the 1990s, for example, negatively impacted real economic activity in the United States because the impaired Japanese banks decreased the volume of their overseas lending, including commercial real estate lending in the

United States. As a result, a "substantial decline in construction activity" in America took place.[7] In the most recent crisis, the interconnection of national economies via multinational enterprises (MNEs) like General Motors and AIG is even more palpable and hence potentially politically disruptive. No matter how necessary to promote global economic stability, an international bailout that appeared to redistribute wealth from the poor of one country to the wealthy of another would be political dynamite. The limited risk of such a redistribution occurring due to the application of Hamilton's Rule, relative to other types of bailouts, is therefore an important additional consideration.

Of course preventing domestic and international crises is preferable to fighting them, a point that banking economist Benton Gup emphasizes in the second chapter, "Financial Crises and Government Responses: Lessons Learned." Gup notes that many financial crises both in the United States and abroad have been caused by the bursting of real estate bubbles, the ill effects of which metastasize to other parts of the financial system and the real economy. The effectiveness of common intervention techniques, including forbearance (doing nothing), provision of short-term liquidity (sometimes via Hamilton's Rule, but more recently at lower rates for all), long-term debt investment, partial or total nationalization, and taxpayer-assisted liquidation, is limited by the fact that they address symptoms rather than causes. Gup persuasively argues that in the future governments should expend more resources trying to prevent crises in the first place by monitoring their typical causes, which include excess leverage, credit risk, interest rate risk, and improper securitization schemes.

In the third chapter, "The Evolution of the Reconstruction Finance Corporation as a Lender of Last Resort in the Great Depression," economist Joseph Mason provides a case study of a bailout gone somewhat but not completely awry. Like the Troubled Assets Relief Program (TARP) bailout created in 2008, the Reconstruction Finance Corporation (RFC) got off to a rocky start. Instead of lending liberally on good collateral as Hamilton's Rule (then known as Bagehot's Rule) suggested, the RFC in 1932, its first year of operation, made loans only to big businesses. Meanwhile the Federal Reserve (the Fed), hampered by the gold standard and its own ideology, also failed to aid safe but liquidity-constrained firms. Both the Fed and the RFC suffered from political squabbling and internecine conflicts, particularly between their New York and Chicago factions.

The public did not like the RFC's conservative lending policies, so its mission was revised in a July 1932 law. The interest rate it charged was lowered, the collateral it demanded relaxed, and its mandate was expanded to include infrastructure projects and exports. The changes, however, did not help the agency stop a major rash of bank failures that fall and in early 1933. Later in 1933, new emergency legislation empowered the RFC to purchase preferred shares and debentures, which helped it to liquidate over 4,000 failed banks and to get almost 13,500 banks into good enough shape to obtain deposit insurance through the new Federal Deposit Insurance Corporation (FDIC) in 1934. By 1935, the RFC had transferred primary responsibility for banking policy to the FDIC and began to wind down its operations, a long process drawn out further by a re-missioning prompted by the government's mobilization for World War II.

Ultimately, the RFC's precise role in resurrecting the U.S. economy in the mid 1930s, if any, is impossible to discern because its specific effects cannot be isolated from those of other New Deal bailouts or the economy's natural resilience. A case can be made, however, that it aided recovery to the extent that it sped up the liquidation of failed banks and prevented additional bank failures.[8] Injections of equity capital through preferred stock purchases worked well in this and other instances and did not unduly burden taxpayers.

In the fourth and final chapter, "After the Storm: The Long-Run Impact of Bank Bailouts," political scientists Guillermo Rosas and Nathan Jensen show that the ambiguity of the RFC's aid is typical of recent government bailouts worldwide. After conducting various statistical analyses, Rosas and Jensen conclude that they cannot reject the hypothesis that government bank bailouts worldwide since 1970 *have not* sped economic recovery. Ascertaining the effects of bailouts on economic output is not an easy exercise, so they are careful not to overdraw their conclusions. Nevertheless, their inability to find compelling statistical evidence of the economic efficacy of bailouts should give policymakers pause. To bail or not to bail is as legitimate a policy question as how to bail out is.

BAILOUTS AND THE CAUSES OF THE CURRENT CRISIS

The devolution of the subprime mortgage crisis of 2007 into the systemic financial crisis of 2008 induced the U.S. government to bail out the financial system and to a lesser extent automakers, taxpayers, and homeowners. Its scattergun approach evinces politicians' natural predisposition to appease as many major constituencies as possible but also reflects a sort of intellectual abyss. The causes of the financial crisis are hotly debated and, if ongoing debates regarding the causes of the Great Depression are any indication, will likely continue to be for years and possibly decades to come. Unfortunately, most discussions are highly, some might say ferociously, partisan. All agree, more or less, about what happened and when. A clear narrative explaining why those events took place, however, remains elusive. That void renders it difficult to create a consensus regarding bailout policy.

Home prices had been rising steadily since the late 1990s but in 2003 began to increase rapidly in markets like Manhattan, Miami, and Southern California. At the same time, banks using new financial techniques greatly expanded mortgage lending to so-called subprime borrowers, individuals who traditionally would not have been able to purchase their homes due to insufficient income, collateral, and/or employment or credit history. Many of the mortgages contained new (or newly rediscovered) features, like interest-only and teaser interest rates scheduled to reset to higher rates in a few years. Soon speculators began taking out subprime mortgages as well, to finance houses they hoped to "flip," or resell, for a profit after a short period. When housing prices were rising, subprime mortgages appeared benign instruments that enriched poor households, real estate speculators, and lenders. Cheap refinancing terms meant that most people who got into trouble could get out of it, at least temporarily, by taking out a new, larger mortgage or adding a second mortgage to an existing one. When housing prices flattened and eventually reversed, however, many of the borrowers defaulted. The poor found it difficult to make payments when the prices of gasoline and other necessities were soaring and easy refinancing disappeared. Speculators found themselves "underwater," owing more on their mortgages than their speculative purchases were worth. The non-performing loans hurt lenders and, through derivatives like mortgage-backed securities, eventually diminished the wealth of numerous investors worldwide.

That caused banks and other lenders to restrict new lending, which ironically led to layoffs and ultimately to more defaults. In 2008, the weight of
numerous defaults led to the failure of several financial companies (Bear
Stearns, Fannie Mae, Freddie Mac, Lehman Brothers, AIG, Washington
Mutual) large and important enough to spark the deepest and most widespread financial panic since the Great Depression.

Why those events occurred depends on who you ask. Generally
speaking, liberals blame the market, while conservatives lambaste the
government. Democrats point to Republican policies, and Republicans
claim all fault falls on Democratic initiatives. Further complicating the
narrative are various fringe groups grinding away at their favorite axes,
like the "culture of consumption" and "greed." No single narrative of
the crisis will satisfy all readers, but I hope in chapter 1 to transcend
the current debate by describing its deep historical and theoretical roots.
Here, my goal is the more modest but still formidable one of narrating
the causes of the crisis from the standpoints of the Left (liberals, Democrats, statists) and the Right (conservatives, Republicans, libertarians).
Both accounts are amalgams, my interpretations of comments made
by scores of bloggers, columnists, policymakers, and TV and talk radio
pundits on both sides of the aisle, and not the views of any particular
persons or groups.[9] No part of either narrative is necessarily wrong in
any absolute sense, but in chapter 1, I'll show that viewing the causes
of the crisis through a partisan lens is bound to make you miss much
of importance — like the crucial role that perverse economic incentives
played at the borrower-lender nexus — and conflate cause, background
condition, and effect.

From the Left, the financial crisis appears to have been rooted in the
actions of unscrupulous financiers who persuaded Congress and presi-
dents Bill Clinton and George W. Bush to deregulate the financial system.
Specifically, financiers won repeal of Glass-Steagall, crucial New Deal
legislation that separated investment banks (which engage in securities
issuance and brokerage and coordinate corporate merger and acquisition
activities) from commercial banks (which take deposits and make loans).
They also changed arcane accounting rules to make it easier to hide their
liabilities in off-balance-sheet entities like the notorious SIVs (special
investment vehicles). Wall Street megabanks also successfully blocked
the Commodity Futures Trade Commission from regulating financial

derivatives that became the basis for massive speculation (risk taking). Those same plutocrats co-opted the Securities and Exchange Commission (SEC), thus undermining another piece of New Deal wisdom that had played a crucial role in maintaining postwar financial and economic stability. Big bankers also managed to cajole global regulators into allowing them to determine their own capital reserve requirements based on their own internal risk assessment models, a practice much akin to hiring a hungry fox to guard a henhouse. Perhaps worst of all, regulators allowed lenders to systematically exploit poor, defenseless borrowers by foisting upon them mortgages and other types of loans that the borrowers could hardly be expected to understand much less repay. Unregulated private mortgage giants Fannie Mae and Freddie Mac exacerbated the situation by aggressively expanding the traditional scope of their business into the subprime mortgage market. Widespread predatory lending practices ultimately undermined the mortgage-backed securities, collateralized mortgage obligations, collateralized debt obligations, and other unregulated derivatives the banks hid in their SIVs. Even as problem loans infected derivatives, which in turn caused massive write downs (accounting losses) at major banks, private credit-rating agencies like Standard and Poor's and Moody's overestimated the quality of mortgage-backed securities and of the firms issuing them, which began to fail in 2008.

To observers on the Right, by contrast, financiers fell victim to inane government regulations and monetary policies. Although once the darling of conservatives, former Federal Reserve chairman Alan Greenspan has been much maligned since the crisis began for keeping interest rates too low for too long toward the end of his tenure. (Apparently, the Right tolerates the Fed when the profits pour in, but when they evaporate at least some on the Right castigate America's central bank as the last bastion of communistic central planning.) Loans contracted between consenting adults cannot be predatory; subprime borrowers could have/should have known what they were getting into. Moreover, before the development of the mortgage-backed securities and off-balance-sheet entities that made subprime lending possible, the government punished banks, via regulations like the Community Reinvestment Act (CRA), for not lending to traditionally underserved groups, including the poor. Although the government did deregulate some aspects of finance, over-regulation remained the largest threat to the financial system's efficient functioning. The SEC, other government regulators, and quasi-government regulators, like the GSEs (government-sponsored enterprises like Fannie and Freddie) and the cartelized and cloistered credit-rating agencies, had sufficient powers of oversight to rein in those few firms that pushed the risk envelope too far. If the market failed, it was for trusting that the massive government regulatory apparatus would do its job and maintain financial system stability. Its inability to do so was not factored into bankers' risk models. Most important, regulators allowed Lehman Brothers to go bankrupt even though financiers had assumed the government would rescue a large, complex company as deeply integrated into a large number of important national and global financial markets as Lehman was. The government then exacerbated the inevitable market chaos that followed with counterproductive emergency measures, like bans on short-selling.

Given its belief that a bumbling government bureaucracy caused the crisis, the Right has naturally exuded more skepticism of the government's bailout efforts, even those initiated by the Republican Bush administration, but some on the Left have also expressed doubts, particularly concerning issues of redistributive fairness. Nevertheless, the U.S. government to date (June 2009) has decided that the crisis warrants bailing out the financial system and domestic automobile manufacturers because both industries are "too big to fail." In other words, their sudden cessation of business would destabilize the economy and cause a systemic crisis that would have long-lasting adverse consequences for all. The fact that distressed financial firms received relatively more money, more quickly, and on easier terms than those offered to Chrysler and General Motors (GM) indicates that policymakers believe that disruption of the financial system poses a substantially larger risk to macroeconomic stability. Many academic researchers concur, noting that financial firms are much more interconnected than manufacturers and provide basic services that few non-financial businesses or consumers can do without. It appears that such claims are correct, at least in this case. After extending short-term emergency loans to the troubled automakers, the government allowed Chrysler to file Chapter 11 bankruptcy on April 30, 2009, and at the time of writing was prepared to allow GM to reorganize under bankruptcy protection as well.[10] The automakers' troubles have led to widespread layoffs at factories and dealerships but have yet to precipitate anything like the panic that gripped the world's financial markets immediately following the bankruptcy of Lehman Brothers on September 15, 2008.

Prior to the fateful decision to allow Lehman to file Chapter 11, the government had underwritten JPMorgan Chase's acquisition of failed investment bank Bear Stearns in mid March 2008, attempted to stimulate the economy over the summer by returning $168 billion to American taxpayers, and on September 6 nationalized giant mortgage banks Fannie Mae and Freddie Mac. Within days after the disruptions caused by the failure of Lehman, the government began to pour what would eventually be over $100 billion into troubled insurer AIG. It also allowed investment banks Goldman Sachs and Morgan Stanley to become bank holding companies so they could obtain emergency liquidity loans from the Federal Reserve. By the end of September, the government had also seized and sold the assets of failed banking giant Washington Mutual to JPMorgan Chase and sketched out an emergency economic stabilization act. After some politically inspired dithering that sent the stock market into a deep downward slide, Congress finally approved the act, and President Bush signed it into law on October 3. The law created the Troubled Asset Relief Program (TARP), a controversial measure initially designed to allow the government to purchase underperforming mortgage-backed securities and other so-called toxic assets. After that plan proved untenable, the government used TARP money to recapitalize banks, many of which partook of the cheap funds until the government began attaching strings to them. The government is also attempting to extend some relief directly to distressed mortgage borrowers, but thus far its efforts in this area have been relatively small and ineffectual.[11]

Meanwhile, the Federal Reserve responded to the crisis by decreasing the effective federal funds rate from 5.25% in mid 2007 to around 3% in early 2008 to close to zero after the Lehman panic, where it remains to this day.[12] It also lent to banks prodigiously via its discount window. When that proved inadequate to meet a variety of demands for cheap loans, it created seven new lending "facilities" designed to ensure the proper functioning of various credit markets. The Term Auction Facility auctions funds to depository institutions, the Primary Dealer Credit Facility provides overnight loans to dealers, the Term Securities Lending

Facility promotes liquidity in the markets for Treasury bonds and other assets typically used as collateral for loans, the Asset-Backed Commercial Paper Money Market Mutual Fund Facility helps banks to purchase high-quality commercial paper from money market funds, the Commercial Paper Funding Facility backstops commercial paper issuers, the Money Market Investor Funding Facility provides liquidity to U.S. money market investors, and the Term Asset-Backed Securities Loan Facility supports the issuance of asset-backed securities collateralized by loans to consumers and businesses.[13]

To justify such massive intervention in the economy, the government raised the specters of rapid financial system meltdown, a massive and potentially sustained decline in economic output, and levels of unemployment not seen since the Great Depression.[14] Only with hindsight can we judge the accuracy of the government's claims and the efficacy of its responses. Already, however, the clearly ad hoc nature of its bailout attempts has created the impression that it was no more prepared for the financial crisis than it was for Hurricane Katrina in 2005. The $2.6 trillion expended on bailouts so far is a sunk cost, water under the proverbial bridge.[15] The important policy question now is how to prevent a recurrence not just of financial crises but of potentially over-exuberant government attempts to rectify the ill effects of any number of potential economic shocks.

POLICY IMPLICATIONS

In terms of future policy, the chapters in this volume collectively suggest the following course:

- Regulators should work much harder to identify and if possible prevent the formation of asset bubbles. That means reducing incentives for risk taking by properly pricing government insurance or other guarantees and reforming the tax system. It also means keeping a close watch on markets for assets that
  - can be shorted or otherwise arbitraged only at great expense;
  - can be purchased with cheap borrowed money;
  - are subject to high agency costs, including poor corporate governance;

- have recently attracted numerous inexperienced participants; or
- are subject to higher levels of risk taking due to the moral hazard created by repeated recent bailouts.[16]

- The Federal Reserve's initial reaction to financial market stringency ought to utilize Hamilton nee Bagehot's Rule rather than lower interest rates for the entire economy. At the same time, money supply growth must be maintained to prevent deflation, even if that means injecting newly created money directly into the economy.

- If a crisis deepens, the government should continue making short-term loans and expanding the money supply but also begin purchasing equity in solvent but stressed financial companies. Instead of an ad hoc process subject to the political process, fear mongering, and emergency conditions, a new or existing agency needs to be empowered to make the equity capital injections, subject of course to specific limits and oversight determined before the next crisis strikes.

- Implementation of either Hamilton's Rule or equity injections should be coordinated internationally, lest MNEs subvert the bailout process by engaging in regulatory arbitrage.[17]

- The government should not protect jobs with tariffs or bailouts of non-financial companies. Rather, it ought to protect family income by offering ample unemployment insurance and other assistance to families that suffer a decline in income through no fault of their own.[18] As the economy improves, the assistance needs to be drawn down so as not to encourage Western European levels of structural unemployment.[19] Again, such policies should be in place before a crisis occurs so they can be designed according to reason and not distorted by partisan politics or fear.

- Likewise, the government should make plans to provide educational and training assistance to workers permanently displaced by the structural economic changes that often occur after crises. Similar programs already in place have already proven woefully inadequate and will undoubtedly be inundated over the next few years.

It would be prudent to enact this course with all deliberate speed to prepare for the next crisis, which the current spate of bailouts may already be creating. Very low interest rates, fast money supply growth, and high levels of moral hazard suggest that a cauldron of inflation and excessive risk taking may be brewing again soon. The better prepared the government is, the less economically, politically, and socially disruptive the next crisis will be.

NOTES

1   Ann Markusen and Joel Yudken, *Dismantling The Cold War Economy* (New York: Basic Books, 1993); and Charles Wolf Jr., *Markets or Governments: Choosing Between Imperfect Alternatives*, 2nd ed. (Cambridge, MA: MIT Press, 1993).

2   John Steinbeck, *The Grapes of Wrath* (1939), not the 1940 movie version, which was toned down considerably.

3   California Department of Water Resources, "California's Drought," http://www.water.ca.gov/drought/.

4   Short introductions to this debate are: Veronique de Rugy, "Stimulating Ourselves to Death," *Reason*, April 2009: 17–18; and the November 2008 exchange between journalist George Will and Nobel economist Paul Krugman on ABC's *This Week* (see "Krugman schools Will" on YouTube: http://www.youtube.com/watch?v=3yAyQV8gOjo).

5   Jean-Charles Rochet and Xavier Vives, "Coordination Failures and the Lender of Last Resort: Was Bagehot Right After All?" *Journal of the European Economic Association* 2, no. 6 (December 2004): 1, 116–47; and Stanley Fischer, "On the Need for an International Lender of Last Resort," *Journal of Economic Perspectives* 13, no. 4 (Autumn 1999): 85–104.

6   Carmen M. Reinhart and Kenneth S. Rogoff, "Banking Crisis: An Equal Opportunity Menace," NBER Working Paper No. 14587 (Cambridge, MA: National Bureau of Economic Research, December 2008).

7   Joe Peek and Eric Rosengren, "Collateral Damage: Effects of the Japanese Bank Crisis on Real Activity in the United States," *American Economic Review* 90, no. 1 (2000): 30–45.

8   Ali Anari, James W. Kolari, and Joseph R. Mason, "Bank Asset Liquidation and the Propagation of the U.S. Great Depression," *Journal of Money, Credit, and Banking* 37, no. 4 (August 2005): 753–73.

9   Those interested in reading the views of some leading commentators in their own words can consult J. Gunnar Trumbull, "The Financial Crisis of 2008," HBS Case No. 709–036 (working paper, Harvard Business School, December 16, 2008), an abstract of which is available here: http://papers.ssrn.com/sol3/papers.cfm?abstract_id=1404546.

10 *Economist*, "Chapter 11 beckons," May 23, 2009, 66–67.

11 For additional details, see the Museum of American Finance's "Tracking the Credit Crisis" exhibit, which can be downloaded here: http://www.moaf.org/exhibits/tracking_the_credit_crisis/index/_res/id=sa_File1/16_CreditCrisis_Spread.pdf.

12 Board of Governors of the Federal Reserve System, "Effective Federal Funds Rate," http://research.stlouisfed.org/fred2/series/FEDFUNDS?cid=118.

13 Board of Governors of the Federal Reserve System, "Monetary Policy," http://www.federalreserve.gov/monetarypolicy/default.htm.

14 For more details, see Kevin Warsh, "The Panic of 2008" (speech, Council of Institutional Investors 2009 Spring Meeting, Washington, DC, April 6, 2009), http://www.federalreserve.gov/newsevents/speech/warsh20090406a.htm.

15 David Goldman, "CNNMoney.com's Bailout Tracker," *CNNMoney.com*, http://money.cnn.com/news/storysupplement/economy/bailouttracker/index.html (accessed May 20, 2009).

16 Dilip Abreu and Markus K. Brunnermeier, "Bubbles and Crashes," *Econometrica* 71, no. 1 (2003): 173–204; Efraim Benmelech, Eugene Kandel, and Pietro Veronesi, "Stock-Based Compensation and CEO (Dis)Incentives," NBER Working Paper No. 13732 (Cambridge, MA: National Bureau of Economic Research, January 2008); Markus K. Brunnermeier and Christian Julliard, "Money Illusion and Housing Frenzies," *Review of Financial Studies* 21, no. 1 (2008): 135–80; Robin Greenwood and Stefan Nagel, "Inexperienced Investors and Bubbles," NBER Working Paper No. 14111 (Cambridge, MA: National Bureau of Economic Research, June 2008); and Charles P. Kindleberger, *Manias, Panics, and Crashes: A History of Financial Crises*, 4th ed. (Hoboken, NJ: Wiley and Sons, 2000).

17 Viral V. Acharya, Paul Wachtel, and Ingo Walter, "International Alignment of Financial Sector Regulation," in *Restoring Financial Stability: How to Repair a Failed System*, ed. Viral V. Acharya and Matthew Richardson (Hoboken, NJ: Wiley, 2009), 365–76.

18 International economists have shown that it is ultimately much cheaper to provide displaced workers with direct subsidies than to keep inefficient companies and industries in operation. Pro-tariff arguments (infant industry, import substitution)

repeatedly have proven themselves empirically wanting. The widespread belief that the early United States industrialized due to protective tariffs is simply wrong, based on mistaken notions of Alexander Hamilton's economic policies. There are a limited number of circumstances in which free trade is suboptimal, but they do not include subsidization of industries that cannot produce at world standards. For an overview, see Thomas A. Pugel, *International Economics*, 12th ed. (New York: McGraw-Hill, 2004). For U.S. industrialization, see Douglas Irwin, "Revenue or Reciprocity? Founding Feuds over Early U.S. Trade Policy," in Douglas Irwin and Richard Sylla, *Founding Choices: American Economic Policy in the 1790s* (Chicago: University of Chicago Press, forthcoming). Chapter drafts can be downloaded here: http://www.nber.org/books/irwi09-1/.

19 On Europe's structural unemployment see, for example, Salvador Ortiguiera, "Unemployment Benefits and the Persistence of European Unemployment" (working paper, European University Institute, Economics Department, February 12, 2002), http://papers.ssrn.com/sol3/papers.cfm?abstract_id=296243; Barbara Petrongolo and Christopher A. Pissarides, "The Ins and Outs of European Unemployment," IZA Working Paper No. 3315 (Bonn, Germany: Institute for the Study of Labor, May 23, 2008), http://papers.ssrn.com/sol3/papers.cfm?abstract_id=1135891; and Georgios C. Bitros and Kyprianos Prodromidis, "Welfare Benefits and the Rate of Unemployment: Some Evidence from the European Union in the Last Thirty Years," Working Paper No. 159 (Athens: Athens University of Economics and Business, May 17, 2005), http://papers.ssrn.com/sol3/papers.cfm?abstract_id=664362.

CHAPTER ONE

Hybrid Failures and Bailouts: Social Costs, Private Profits

ROBERT E. WRIGHT

Economic and financial crises are one of the costs of reaping the benefits of living in a market economy. The frequency, magnitude, and severity of crises, however, are not predetermined and can be lessened with proper public policies and market behaviors. In addition, government can to a large extent control which parties will bear crisis costs. Determining the costs that ought to fall on individuals, on businesses, or on society at large is a difficult task not attempted in this chapter, which limits itself to the proposition that if the profits of a risky enterprise accrue to private entities, the costs created by said enterprise ought to as well. Some government-funded bailouts in the United States and elsewhere have violated that proposition by socializing the costs created by risky enterprises without a commensurate socialization of profit. Such policies strike many observers as unfair. More important, they are counterproductive because they increase the likelihood of crisis by enticing businesses to assume large risks.

Crises and bailouts are not the only hyper-dysfunctional parts of modern economies, but all appear rooted in what I term hybrid failures — complicated combinations of market and government failures that render the many difficulties that nature imposes on humanity largely intractable. Upon being cast out of paradise, humanity was forever forced to confront the great banes of existence: scarcity, asymmetric information, uncertainty, and risk. Scarcity necessitates rationing, be it by price, quantity, time, or some other criterion. Asymmetric information (adverse selection, moral hazard, agency problems) complicates lending, insurance, and governance, inside both the firm and the polity. Uncertainty weighs upon humans and their institutions like a tax of unknown and unknowable size and duration. Risk, the probability that an outcome will deviate from expectations, cajoles some people into combat because they believe it can be tamed. Scarcity, asymmetric information, and uncertainty conspire against the optimists, however, while rent seekers run amok, earning private profits in the halcyon years but transferring their losses onto society during inclement times.

The religious allusion is apropos; risk management has a hoary history steeped in religion. For eons, forecasting the future was almost exclusively the purview of oracles and priests. Only within the last few hundred years has the management of risk become a scientific venture. In fact, according to Peter Bernstein, "the revolutionary idea that defines the boundary between modern times and the past is the mastery of risk: the notion that the future is more than a whim of the gods and that men and women are not passive before nature."[1] But even after reason trumped faith, religion and risk remained closely associated. Religious leaders saw that insuring against risk could increase moral hazard, inciting people to burn their homes or kill themselves or others for the love of lucre. To this day, religious organizations provide risk mitigation services in a valiant but only partially successful attempt to fill the yawning gap between private and public risk management.

Risk is a bad and its management a good, and a scarce one at that, so it comes at a cost that somebody must bear. The cost of bearing risk, or the cost of its management, can be paid privately, by individuals or their agents (insurers, for example), or socially, by the government and/ or churches, charities, and other NGOs (non-governmental organizations). Typically, private risk bearers try to socialize the cost of risk to induce some societal group, usually the government, to pick up the tab.[2] Social risk bearers, by contrast, often display mixed motives. Sometimes, especially in the wake of emergencies like the terrorist attacks in 2001, they are willing and able to take on the cost. At other times, they are willing to assume risks but unable to do so due to budget and borrowing constraints. Sometimes, they are financially able to bear the risks but unwilling to do so for political, ideological, religious, or other reasons. Sometimes, they are neither willing nor able to assume private risks and may even seek to re-impose previously socialized risks back onto individuals.

According to business historian David Moss, the U.S. government has been socializing risk since its inception. Until about 1900 it tried to stimulate economic growth by protecting businesses from risks with policies like limited liability, bankruptcy law, and the gold standard. From 1900 until about 1960, the government tried to provide security for workers with workers' compensation laws, unemployment programs, Social Security, and the like. Since 1960, Moss argues, the government has tried to provide security for all, including consumers, homeowners, credit card holders, and numerous other interest groups.[3] In the last decade or so, however, the government has increased the risks individuals must bear for unemployment, health care, disaster relief, and other previously socialized risks while simultaneously sheltering risky businesses with public funds.[4] As table 1.1 reveals, government reaction to domestic economic distress ranges across a wide spectrum from doing nothing to full-scale nationalization.[5] Combinations also occur. For example, the purchase and assumption agreements the Federal Deposit Insurance Corporation (FDIC) uses to sell failed banks to solvent institutions often include government guarantees.[6]

Observers typically label as a bailout any government action on behalf of a distressed company or industry (see items 2–10 in table 1.1). That is likely because the action noun "bailout" stems from the complex verb "to bail out," which evokes three different images: of a prisoner being released after posting bond, of water being dumped from a sinking boat, and of a pilot jumping out of a damaged aircraft. None of those images are particularly analogous to any type of government bailout, but all share the notion of rescue from a bad situation. As scarce goods, rescues are costly. The Risk column of table 1.1 indicates whether society or private parties bear the risks and other costs associated with different types of bailouts. The Profits column, by contrast, indicates who directly benefits from the government intervention.

Non-intervention and private bailouts pose no direct difficulties because private profits are earned on the basis of private risk taking. The

REACTION	RISK	PROFITS	EXAMPLES
1a. do nothing—won't	Not socialized: government does not feel that it is appropriate or prudent to do so	Private	Enron, 2001 Superior Bank, 2001 Lehman Brothers, 2008
1b. do nothing—can't	Not socialized: government is unable to do so for ideological and/or institutional reasons	Private	Banking crises in 1819, 1837–39, 1857, 1873, 1884, 1893–95
2. broker a private rescue	Not socialized: government uses its power to induce private parties to aid troubled companies	Private	J. P. Morgan, 1907 National Credit Corporation, 1931 Long-Term Capital Management, 1998
3. favoritism	Not socialized: government endows troubled companies with a competitive advantage, such as a protective tariff or regulatory forbearance	Private	Bank holiday of 1933 Life insurer forbearance, 1930s Savings and loan crisis, Phase 1 Steel tariffs, 2002
4. cash grants	Socialized: government directly subsidizes distressed entities with cash	Private	Airline industry, 2001 merger sweetener (cash to acquirer) payoff (cash to uninsured creditors)
5. loan guarantees	Socialized: government guarantees the debts of troubled companies	Depends on details	Lockheed, 1971 Chrysler, 1979 GSEs
6a. lender of last resort— modern central bank rule	Socialized: government loans to distressed companies and industries with indifferent collateral at a subsidized rate	Mostly private	Stock market crash, 1987 Currency and sovereign default crisis, 1997–98 Y2K, dot-com bubble burst, 9/11, 1999–2002 Subprime mortgage crisis, 2007
6b. lender of last resort— Hamilton nee Bagehot's Rule	Socialized: government loans to distressed companies on good collateral at a penalty rate	Mostly public	Panic of 1792 Reconstruction Finance Corporation, Phase 1
7. troubled asset purchases	Socialized: government purchases the troubled or illiquid assets of distressed companies	Private/public	FDIC assumption of bad bank debts TARP, Phase 1
8. equity investor of last resort (partial nationalization)	Socialized: government purchases equity stakes in distressed companies	Private/public	Reconstruction Finance Corporation, Phase 2 Continental Illinois, 1984 TARP, Phase 2
9. conservatorship	Socialized: government owns bankrupt companies with the intent of winding down their operations and selling their assets in a controlled fashion	Public	Bridge banks, e.g., First Republic Bank of Texas, 1988 Resolution Trust Corporation, 1989 Fannie Mae and Freddie Mac, 2008
10. full nationalization	Socialized: government owns troubled companies with the intent of owning and operating them, though it may privatize them later	Public	Conrail, 1976–87 Amtrak, 1971–ongoing

Source: Author based on Benton E. Gup, ed., *Too Big to Fail: Policies and Practices in Government Bailouts* (Westport, CT: Praeger, 2004); Benton E. Gup, ed., *International Banking Crises: Large-Scale Failures, Massive Government Interventions* (Westport, CT: Quorum Books, 1999); and Irvine H. Sprague, *Bailout: An Insider's Account of Bank Failures and Rescues* (New York: Basic Books, 1986).

Table 1.1   Spectrum of government bailouts

problem is that those responses may not be sufficient to stem financial crises and economic recessions, which are socially costly. Favoritism that takes the form of monopolies or tariffs may socialize costs by passing them onto consumers (rather than taxpayers per se). Regulatory forbearance can create large costs in the future, as in the savings and loan crisis, but can also be salutary, as when regulators eased accounting rules for life insurers during the Great Depression.[7] Cash grants socialize risks by making direct transfers from taxpayers to companies and other economic entities, such as the uninsured creditors of failed banks. (Insured creditors, by contrast, receive a subsidy only to the extent that deposit insurance premiums are too low.)[8] Their only justification is to stop major economic disruptions. Loan guarantees socialize risk, but if they are priced appropriately they need not create private profits. It is not clear if the government charged Lockheed and Chrysler enough for the guarantees that they received in the 1970s, but the companies repaid, and taxpayers profited. The implicit guarantee of the bonds of Fannie Mae and Freddie Mac, by contrast, led to billions of dollars of taxpayer losses and the emolument of private stockholders for over three decades.

Lender-of-last-resort actions by modern central banks have also led to mostly private profits supported by socialized risks. When faced with macroeconomic shocks and financial crises, modern central banks lower key bank interest rates in order to flood the market with liquidity, ease credit tensions, and so forth. Sometimes borrowers' rates also decline but usually not as much as the cost of banks' funds (overnight loans from other banks, loans from the central bank itself, deposits, negotiable certificates of deposit) do. In other words, easy monetary policy increases banks' gross spread, making them more profitable and less likely to fail. With such policies, modern central banks essentially reward bankers and other financiers for disrupting the financial system.[9]

Under Hamilton's Rule, developed by Alexander Hamilton during the Panic of 1792 and rediscovered by the Bank of England in the nineteenth century, central banks during panics raised the interest rate (above the prevailing rate under normal circumstances, but much less than market rates during the panic) but lent to anybody who wanted to borrow and could post sufficient collateral. The notion was that companies that had taken on excessive risks would fail but all solid companies would be able to put up sufficient collateral to survive. The collateral and the high rate of interest meant that socialization of risk, while still present, was minimized and most of the profits accrued to the central bank. Hamilton's Rule also minimized moral hazard because risky companies expected to fail and nobody expected to profit from adverse market conditions.

Government purchase of troubled assets and partial nationalization (equity investor of last resort) may also be structured so that potential public profits are commensurate with the risks that the government assumes on behalf of taxpayers during the bailout process. The partial nationalization of failed bank Continental Illinois, for example, made the government a profit of almost $100 million, which might have been fair compensation for the risk incurred.[10] Other bailouts, however, have redistributed significant amounts of wealth from taxpayers to bailout recipients' employees, creditors, and/or stockholders.[11]

Conservatorship and full-blown nationalization usually align social risks and social profits quite closely. Liquidating a failed business is relatively easy, so the government generally does it tolerably well. Government ownership and operation of complex going concerns, by contrast, often leads to inefficient political decision making and substantial operating losses, as with Amtrak.[12] For that reason, many policymakers oppose full nationalization but tolerate conservatorship and equity-investor-of-last-resort actions.

Regardless of whether the public profits or not, taxpayers often construe bailouts as private interest legislation that comes at their expense, as "handouts" to undeserving parties.[13] They are correct to the extent that bailouts allow some companies to engage in highly remunerative but risky activities safe in the knowledge that the government will provide aid if they suffer large losses. Those companies keep their profits in good times but in bad times pass their losses, or at least the prospect of losses, onto taxpayers. That, of course, is anathema to the widespread belief that businesses should assume private risks in exchange for private profits that they share with society via the tax system.[14]

How some private companies came to earn almost riskless private profits is the subject of this chapter. The first section, "Government Failures," describes major types of government failures and establishes that many sectors of the U.S. economy are hyper-dysfunctional. The second section, "Market and Hybrid Failures," describes major types of market failures and explains that most hyper-dysfunctional aspects of the economy are the result of intricate combinations of both market *and* government failures. "Socialization of Risk and Privatization of Profit: Historical Origins," the third section, describes how two centuries of hybrid failures culminated in the messed-up mortgage market of 2007 and the botched bailout of 2008. The third section also proffers several major policy reform recommendations designed to reduce the probability of a crisis recurrence but suggests that uncertainty, risk, and the other banes of human existence likely will prove virulent enough to cause financial panics in the future. In response to those crises, policymakers will need to weigh the benefits of stabilizing the macroeconomy against the costs of increasing moral hazard and exacerbating dysfunction-inducing hybrid failures. If a bailout is deemed necessary, the government should invoke Hamilton's Rule or otherwise try to ensure that it does not promote excessive risk taking.[15]

GOVERNMENT FAILURES

In terms of the inflation-adjusted value of final physical goods and services that the average American produces in a year (in the language of economists, real per capita gross domestic product), the U.S. economy is among the best in the world and has been for two centuries. Since World War II, American labor productivity (inflation-adjusted value of output per hour worked) has more than trebled.[16] It may seem strange to call such an economy hyper-dysfunctional, yet the American economy's success is relative, not absolute, and most people sense that inefficient institutions, sagging sectors, and problematic policies produce considerable drag.

Simultaneously socializing risk and privatizing profit for a handful of mega-corporations is perhaps the worst policy of all, but other hyper-dysfunctional aspects of the economy abound. (Space precludes an in-depth analysis of these complex issues here, but interested readers can consult my forthcoming book *Fubarnomics* and the other sources cited in the chapter notes for details.) According to Auburn University's David Schramm, divorce creates $33 billion per year in deadweight costs for the U.S. economy.[17] Health care and retirement savings, including Social Security and private pensions, also create large losses due to inefficiencies and mis-aligned incentives. Likewise, the custom construction industry is hyper-dysfunctional. Despite technological advances, construction productivity is no higher now than half a century ago, and a large percentage of construction projects end up over budget, overdue, or under quality, and sometimes all three.[18]

The processes by which we buy, sell, and insure the titles of our homes are also hyper-dysfunctional. Not one but two cartels distort the market for homes. As New York University economist Lawrence White has shown, real estate agents fix prices (and their 6% commissions) well above the likely market rate, especially for more expensive homes.[19] Another cartel, recently exposed in a book published by New York University Press, takes billions a year out of the pockets of homeowners under the sobriquet "title insurance."[20]

Higher education is another lagging sector where productivity, as far as anyone can tell, is stagnant. Tuition and other costs rise faster than inflation; complaints about low quality are numerous and for the most part well founded. American higher education is arguably the best in the world, but that does not mean that U.S. universities and colleges are any good, only that foreign ones are even worse. Higher education has been in perpetual crisis for the last several decades. Tuition rates soared in inflation-adjusted terms, forcing students to borrow or work instead of study. Standards plummeted, while grade "inflation" (actually compression) led to ridiculous outcomes, like three-quarters of classes graduating with "honors." Businesses meantime found that they had to engage in unprecedented amounts of corporate training.[21]

The United States appears headed down an unhappy path trodden by many before it. The late, great University of Maryland economist Mancur Olson argued that as a country's political structure reifies or ages, its economy becomes sclerotic due to the accumulated weight of special-interest legislation, of the ever-increasing number of laws enacted to aid the few at the expense of the many.[22] The American economy is no exception. From Washington, D.C., congressman John Murtha ensures that "pork," in the form of government contracts, pours into his district in western Pennsylvania. Many of the federal contracts that Murtha's favorite Johnstown-area firms win are "no-bid" deals. In other words, the companies face no competition, virtually ensuring that they reap large profits, ill-gotten gains taken directly from taxpayers' pockets.

Worse, many of those contracts are for goods or services that *no* branch of the military or government agency actually wants or requested. If one of Murtha's favored firms makes it, the government gets it, whether it wants it or not.[23]

Similarly, with the post-Katrina cleanup still far from finished, Senator Stevens of Alaska tried to divert over $200 million to build a bridge to connect a small Alaskan town to a tiny island inhabited by about fifty people. "The Bridge to Nowhere," as critics dubbed it, was snubbed even by locals who had gotten around quite well for generations by boat and airplane. (Small private planes are ubiquitous in Alaska.)[24] Were Murtha and Stevens renegade exceptions to the rule, there would be little to worry about. Unfortunately, almost everyone in Congress relishes such pork, or "earmarks" as they have come to be known.

Bureaucrats, from the recalcitrant clerk at the Department of Motor Vehicles to a GS-15 Step 10 (the top of the federal government's "general schedule" of pay), are also major contributors to dysfunction. Governments fail, or help create dysfunctional conditions, for a variety of reasons. Foremost, as noted in the introduction, reality is unkind. Only with considerable effort can the best and the brightest barely fathom its shadowy depths. Information about how the world works is scarce and imperfect, and the future looms uncertain and foreboding. Systems are chaotic in the sense that small changes in initial conditions can lead to large differences in outcomes. A seemingly small policy change can ripple through the economy, destroying equilibrium the way a tossed pebble wreaks havoc on the surface of a placid pond. Unlike the pond, however, the economy doesn't necessarily return to its former state. Rather, like a human face, it may forever bear the scar created by the ill-conceived rock's shock.[25]

Governments also fail because they are composed of fallible people. Sometimes their foibles induce them to make very well-intentioned mistakes. More often, though, their flaws lead them to satisfy their own wishes and purses instead of those of the people they ostensibly serve. In some countries, including the United States, private interestedness is checked by elections or other parts of the government—the independent judiciary, the bicameral legislature, federalism, and all that. Self-interested behavior still pervades public life, but it is more muted than in Stalin's Soviet Union or Mugabe's Zimbabwe. Instead of outright theft, American politicians and bureaucrats engage in more oblique, and hence in some ways more insidious, self-serving activities. Earmarks, campaign contributions, vote swapping, work slowdowns, extra-long lunches, Luddite-like resistance to technology, and self-serving regulatory forbearance are only a few such behaviors.[26]

Government employees are not inherently incompetent but rather respond to incentives — or more usually, the lack of them. As Milton Friedman once pointed out, the savviest, most efficient private sector manager or worker will morph into a stereotypical bureaucrat soon after taking up public sector employment.[27] The root problem is that governments need not worry about output, or actual outcomes. Whether the government succeeds or fails, its collectors are still going to knock on taxpayers' doors and break them in if necessary. In fact, if the government fails it may well ask for yet higher taxes! Johnny will be able to read, or Mary won't get raped, or Widow Smith won't perish cold and hungry, or al Qaeda will be defeated if only the taxman digs a little deeper into citizens' pockets, or so politicians often claim. There are limits, of course. A government that exacts high taxes and provides little in return faces a higher chance of coup, rebellion, or revolution. But bad governments do not always face negative repercussions. Consider Cuba and North Korea, the citizens of which for decades have groaned under authoritarian poverty.

Unlike for-profit enterprises, governments face no immediate sanctions for profligacy or inefficiency. Also unlike private enterprises, at least those in competitive markets with good internal incentive compatibility, parts of the government work at cross-purposes with other parts for extended periods of time.[28] Such discrepancies are usually unplanned, arising from conflicting special interests and the remnants of piecemeal policy prescriptions enacted over decades or centuries. For example, the U.S. government long simultaneously subsidized tobacco farmers and tried to reduce cigarette consumption through taxes, bans, and public education. Government-sponsored agricultural R&D (research and development) increased output and hence depressed agricultural prices at the same time that other government programs sought to increase them. Programs that paid farmers not to grow crops decreased farm employment, forcing itinerant workers onto the dole or worse. Even more tragically, during the Depression some parts of the government burned crops (to raise agricultural prices to help farmers) while other parts struggled to obtain enough food to nourish the unemployed.[29]

Because the government does not have to worry very much about outcomes, it provides employees with salaries based on their test scores or years of experience and not on how well they service taxpayers. Lifetime employment is almost guaranteed. Bonuses are rarely paid for saving taxpayers' money. Suggesting radical changes will earn a bureaucrat not laurels but a one-way ticket to a dead-end position in a cold, dangerous, or faraway post.

Government inefficiencies and failures persist because no one has sufficient incentive to make the government more efficient, to maximize its output or minimize its input. More is at stake here than just efficiency, though. When governments fail, the results are often spectacularly horrifying. Governments are among the leading causes of war, famine, and pestilence. (Organized religions are close behind, especially when they assume the trappings of government, as in medieval Europe and other theocracies.) Like any powerful tool, government can unleash great good but also great evil. It sometimes improves the performance of the hyperdysfunctional parts of the economy, but more often it exacerbates existing problems and sows the seeds of future calamities.

MARKET AND HYBRID FAILURES

Were government the only cause of economic dysfunction, the proper course of action would be to limit its power. Unfortunately, the world is not so simple, not by a long shot. Just as governments can fail, so too can markets. As noted previously, humans are subject to scarcity and asymmetric information. The former means that opportunity costs rule. People cannot have their cake and eat it too. Doing A necessitates foregoing B. To buy guns (military protection), the taxpayer must give up butter (consumer goods), and vice versa. Scarcity makes markets possible, nay necessary. People cannot have everything that they desire, so they must have some way of rationing goods.[30]

In their purest form, as described in words by Adam Smith and in mathematics by Kenneth Arrow and others, markets are elegant ways of coping with scarcity. People still do not have everything that they want, but they do have ways of efficiently deciding what, where, when, and how much to produce and of distributing those goods in an ostensibly fair manner, with those who produce the most receiving the most in return. Were scarcity humanity's only problem, life would almost be easy.

Asymmetric information, however, blindsides markets, smashing Smith's words and Arrow's equations to bits. When people complain about markets, they almost always are really complaining about asymmetric information, or to be more precise, its negative effects on the way that markets function. In the Smith-Arrow world, everyone knows everything, or at least everything they need in order to avoid getting cheated by others. Markets establish prices at just the point where producers recoup their costs of production and earn enough profit to keep them in business. Consumers know what those prices are and can tell high-quality goods from low-quality ones. Workers' wages equal their marginal productivity, so no one is under- or overpaid and nobody shirks and gets away with it.

In the real world, the one suffused with asymmetric information, the pretty Smith-Arrow outcomes rarely occur. Consumers pay too much for substandard products; some workers earn more than they produce, and others earn much less; and companies come to have market power, the ability to *make* prices rather than to *take* them from the market as in perfectly competitive systems. With asymmetric information comes power, the ability to lie, cheat, and steal one's way to outsized profits. It's a two-way street too. Sometimes businesses entice investors into buying overpriced financial securities (stocks, bonds, derivatives). Sometimes consumers trick banks into lending them money that they will never repay or insurers into paying fraudulent claims. None of this is the fault of markets per se but rather asymmetric information in all three of its facets: adverse selection, moral hazard, and agency problems.

The classic case of adverse selection is the market for "lemons," which is to say breakdown-prone automobiles. People who offer lemons for sale know that their cars are subpar. Most automobile buyers, however, cannot tell if a car is prone to breakdown. They might kick the tires, take it for a short spin, look under the hood, and whatnot, all without discovering the truth. The seller has superior information and indeed has an incentive to increase the asymmetry by hiding any obvious problems. She might thoroughly warm the car up before showing it to prospective buyers, put high-quality gasoline in the tank, clean up oil spots in the driveway, and so forth. She may even lie about the automobile's history and provenance. The buyer offers the average price for used cars of the particular make, model, year, and mileage. The seller accepts, but a day, week, month, or year later, the buyer learns that he has overpaid for his automotive lemon. He complains to his relatives, friends, and neighbors, many of whom tell similar horror stories. They decide that all used cars are lemons.

Of course, some used cars are actually very reliable "peaches." A peach owner, however, cannot credibly inform potential buyers of the car's quality. She can tell the truth about the car, but how can the buyer be sure she isn't lying? So the asymmetric information remains, and the hapless buyer offers the average price for used cars of the particular make, model, year, and mileage. But this time the seller declines the offer as too low. The buyer's relatives, friends, and neighbors were partly correct. Not all used cars for sale are lemons, but those that actually change hands are!

The lemons story is a simple but powerful one. With appropriate changes, it applies to everything from investment advice to construction services to bonds. Because of asymmetric information, lenders cannot ration on price. As the interest rate increases, the best borrowers drop out of the bidding because they know that their projects are safe, that they are the equivalent of an automotive peach. People with riskier business projects continue bidding until they too find the cost of borrowing too high and bow out, leaving the bank to lend to a knave, to some human lemon, at a very high rate of interest that will never be paid. Adverse selection also afflicts the market for insurance. Safe businesses are not willing to pay much for insurance because they know that the likelihood that they will suffer a loss and make a claim is low. Risky businesses, by contrast, will pay high rates for insurance because they know that they will probably suffer a loss. Those planning on burning the insured property at the first opportunity will offer to pay a very high premium indeed! Anyone offering insurance on the basis of premium alone will end up getting hurt, just as the lender who rations on price alone will.

Adverse selection is pre-contractual asymmetric information; moral hazard is post-contractual asymmetric information. It occurs whenever a borrower or insured entity (not an applicant, an actual borrower or policyholder) engages in behaviors that are not in the best interest of the lender or insurer. Moral hazard occurs when a borrower uses a bank loan to buy lottery tickets instead of safe government bonds or an insured leaves the door of his home or car unlocked, lets candles burn all night unattended, or fakes an accident. Such behavior is called moral hazard because it was long thought to indicate a lack of morals or character. In a sense it does, but thinking about an information problem in moralistic terms does not help to mitigate it because most people will engage in immoral activities for personal gain if given the chance. It is extremely tempting to put other people's money at risk. As discussed below, increased moral hazard is one of the major causes of financial crises and one of the major costs of bailouts.[31]

The principal-agent problem, an important sub-category of moral hazard that involves post-contractual asymmetric information of a specific type, is another major cause of financial crises. Most of the time, principals (owners) must appoint agents (employees) to conduct some or all of their business affairs on their behalf. Stockholders in joint-stock corporations, for example, hire professional executives to run their businesses. The executives hire middle managers, who in turn hire supervisors, who then hire employees. The principal-agent problem arises when any of those agents does not act in the best interest of the principal, for example when employees or managers steal, slack off, act rudely toward customers, or otherwise cheat the company's owners.

The monitoring of agents (supervising of employees) helps to mitigate the principal-agent problem. Another, often more powerful way of reducing agency problems is to try to align the incentives of employees with those of owners by paying efficiency wages, commissions, bonuses, stock options, and the like. Caution is the watchword here, however, because people typically do *precisely* what they are given incentives to do. Failure to recognize that apparently universal human trait has had adverse consequences for numerous organizations. A major ice cream retailer decided to help out its employees by allowing them to consume, free of charge, any mistakes they might make in the course of serving customers. What was meant to be a little perk turned into a major problem as employee waistlines bulged and profits shrank because hungry employees found it easy to make delicious frozen mistakes.

Similarly, a debt collection agency almost destroyed itself by agreeing to change the way that it compensated its collectors. Initially, collectors received bonuses based on the dollars collected divided by the dollars assigned to be collected. For example, a collector who brought in $250,000 of the $1 million due on his accounts would receive a bigger bonus than a collector who brought in only $100,000 of the same denominator ($250/1,000 = .25 > 100/1,000 = .10$). Collectors complained, however, that it was not fair to them if one or more of their accounts went bankrupt, rendering collection impossible. The managers of the collection agency agreed and began to deduct the value of bankrupt accounts from the collectors' denominators. Under the new incentive scheme, a collector who brought in $100,000 would receive a bigger bonus than his colleague if, say, $800,000 of his accounts claimed bankruptcy ($100/[1,000 - 800 = 200] = .5 > 250/1,000 = .25$). The collectors quickly transformed themselves into bankruptcy counselors because the new scheme inadvertently created a perverse incentive, that is, one diametrically opposed to the collection agency's interest, which was to collect as many dollars as possible, not to help debtors file for bankruptcy.

In a competitive market, pressure from competitors and the incentives of managers would soon rectify such mishaps. But when the incentive structure of management is deranged, bigger and deeper problems often appear. For example, managers paid with stock options have incentives to increase stock prices. They almost invariably succeed in getting their stock up, sometimes by making their companies more efficient but sometimes, as investors in the U.S. stock market in the late 1990s learned, through accounting legerdemain.[32]

Improperly aligned incentives also help to explain other market failures, including collective action problems and externalities. Sometimes, people would be better off if they all contributed to some cause, like national defense. Rather than everybody pitching in, however, people have incentives to "free ride," to let others contribute while they pay nothing but still enjoy the protection of the armed forces. Because of rampant free riding, goods that are nonrivalrous and nonexcludable, goods that people cannot be prevented from enjoying even if they have not pitched in to pay for them, must be provided by the government if they are to be provided at all. For that reason, economists call them public goods.

Externalities occur when the costs or benefits of a good are not fully internalized by the market. Education is the classic example of a positive externality. Society reaps extra benefits from educated people in the form of better dinner guests, less crime, innovation spillovers, and the like. Because individuals do not gain from those extra benefits, the argument goes, they acquire less education than is socially optimal. The government should therefore subsidize education to ensure that individuals obtain more of it, not for their own sake, but for society's. Pollution presents the opposite case, the classic example of a negative externality. Because factory owners do not have to pay for the problems their factories cause downstream, downwind, or later in time, they can sell their goods more cheaply. That means that people buy more units, encouraging additional production and hence more pollution. Large, complex financial institutions also create a type of pollution or negative externality, systemic financial fragility. They also contribute to the creation of asset bubbles, the leading cause of financial crises.

Characterized by rapid increases in the value of some asset, like stocks or real estate, asset bubbles are usually fueled by some combination of low interest rates, new technology, increases in demand, and leverage (borrowing). They become market failures when the price of the asset detaches from underlying fundamentals and becomes driven by the expectation that the price will continue to rise long enough for it to be sold at a profit. The rapid increase in U.S. housing prices in the early third millennium was a classic bubble.[33]

Were markets the only problem we faced, we would be wise to give the government more power to regulate them. Unfortunately, as we learned above, the government's failures are as pervasive as the market's. Supplanting markets with governments, as communist countries did, led to nothing but economic disasters that killed millions of people and maimed the lives and limbs of millions more. Balancing between government and market is not a solution, either. In fact, hyper-dysfunctional aspects of the economy are usually the product of both government and market failures, or what are termed here hybrid failures. Complex layering of government and market failures has increased divorced rates and health care, retirement, education, and construction costs. Hybrid failures also lie at the heart of the housing bubble, subprime mortgage crisis, and questionable bailouts of 2008–9, partisan claims to the contrary notwithstanding. While statists and commentators on the left focused blame on market failures and libertarians and those from the right pointed primarily to government failures, an insidiously more complex reality lurked beneath.[34]

SOCIALIZATION OF RISK AND PRIVATIZATION OF PROFIT: HISTORICAL ORIGINS

Even before the United States was born, the colonists of British North America faced numerous financial difficulties, including the real estate bubble of the 1760s. During the French and Indian War (1754–63), the colonial economy boomed because the British armed forces expended large sums, privateering (essentially legal pirating against enemy ships) and smuggling were lucrative, and colonial legislatures pumped out money (called bills of credit) in prodigious quantities to fund the war effort. Internationally traded goods were tethered to the world price level, itself a function of the world supply and demand of gold and silver, so their prices increased relatively modestly in the colonies during the war. The prices of non-traded goods like wages and real estate, by contrast, soared, doubling and even tripling. The extraordinary prices were clearly a temporary aberration, an asset bubble. Nevertheless, throughout the colonies many people borrowed large sums at low interest rates to buy farms, urban lots, and town homes.[35]

In 1764, a great reversal took place. With the war over, British spending dropped precipitously, privateering and smuggling profits evaporated, taxes swelled, and the money supply decreased rapidly. Not surprisingly, interest rates spiked and wages and real estate prices plummeted. After one or two years, most mortgages became callable, a contractual arrangement that allowed lenders to demand repayment of their principal. In the mid 1760s, lenders called en masse so they could re-invest their principal at higher rates and because most properties no longer fully collateralized the mortgages they backed. Most borrowers could not repay or refinance and ended up losing their farms, shops, and homes. Many ended up in debtors' prison. Rather than ameliorate the situation by allowing colonists to trade more freely internationally, to pay off their war debts more slowly, and to reduce their taxes, the British government did the exact opposite and imposed the Sugar, Currency, and

Stamp acts. Greatly angered, the colonists resisted the Stamp Act, setting off a course of events that culminated in revolution and independence.

Well aware that macroeconomic instability and government intractability could foment another rebellion, Alexander Hamilton, America's first treasury secretary under the Constitution of 1787, devised institutions that empowered the government to alleviate financial panics. In addition to stockpiling Treasury bonds in an institution called the "Sinking Fund," Hamilton created a private central bank, called the Bank of the United States, which held the government's deposits and, when necessary, lent it money. (The central bank also regulated state banks by returning their notes to them for redemption in gold and silver, thereby inducing them to hold safe levels of cash reserves.) In the late winter and early spring of 1792, Hamilton used these mechanisms, along with a timely foreign loan, to stop a financial panic stemming from the deflation of a bubble in government bonds. In the process, he divined the policy rule, later commonly known as Bagehot's Rule, that during crises governments should lend prodigiously at a penalty rate to all comers who can post sufficient collateral. Loans were expensive and collateralized to ensure that taxpayers were protected from loss and that distressed borrowers felt economic pain instead of gain. It worked. Instead of suffering from years of political instability and possibly rebellion, the U.S. economy grew robustly and did not face another major peacetime financial panic until 1819.[36]

The very success of Hamilton's Rule, however, was its undoing. By the time the next crisis struck, Hamilton and other key players had died or retired. In addition, technological improvements made the specie standard tighter, eliminating much of the wiggle room that Hamilton had used in 1792 to temporarily increase the money supply and stave off the panic. Nicholas Biddle, president of the (second) Bank of the United States, successfully thwarted, in 1825, the spread of a financial panic from Britain. With that central bank's demise in 1836 and the elimination of the Sinking Fund with repayment of the national debt in 1834, however, the government no longer had the tools needed to fight the ill effects of the financial panics that struck in 1837–39, 1857, 1873, 1884, 1893–95, and 1907. (It did grant subsidies of questionable necessity to transatlantic steamship lines, telegraph companies, railroads, and other favored enterprises, but most such transfers were justified using the rhetoric of development rather than emergency bailout.)[37]

CRISIS YEAR(S)	CAUSES	RECESSION YEARS	REAL PER CAPITA GDP HIGH (2000 USD)	REAL PER CAPITA GDP LOW (2000 USD)	PERCENTAGE DECLINE (%)	EFFECTS
1837–39	Real estate; agriculture; canals	1837–43	$1,681	$1,618	4	Wave of state constitutional reforms
1857	Grain; gold	1857–58	$2,252	$2,202	2	Republican party solidification and increased sectional animosity
1873	Railroad securities; real estate	1873–79	$2,834	$2,737	3	Rise of labor unions and agrarian reform groups
1893–95	Railroad and other equities	1893–97	$4,559	$3,913	14	Populism; Progressivism; Great Merger Movement
1907	Equities	1907–8	$5,621	$4,917	12.5	Federal Reserve System
1929–33	Equities; banks; real estate	1929–33	$7,099	$5,056	29	RFC (1932); FDIC (1933); SEC (1933); SSA (1935)
1980s	Savings and loans; real estate	1980–82	$23,007	$22,346	3	FIRREA and RTC (1989); Riegle-Neal (1994)
		1990–91	$28,429	$28,007	1.5	
2000–1	Equities; corporate accounting	2001	$34,759	$34,659	.02	Sarbanes-Oxley (2002)
2007–?	Real estate; subprime mortgages; derivatives	2008–?	$38,148	$??,???	??	Emergency Economic Stabilization Act (2008); ??

Source: Author based on Robert E. Wright, "Financial crisis and reform: Looking back for clues to the future," *McKinsey Quarterly Online*, December 2008, http://www.mckinseyquarterly.com/Financial_crisis_and_reform_Looking_back_for_clues_to_the_future_2271. Post-1857 recession dates are from the National Bureau of Economic Research, "Business Cycle Expansions and Contractions," http://www.nber.org/cycles.html. Real per capita GDP statistics to 1790 are from Measuring Worth, "What Was the US GDP Then: Annual Observations in Table and Graphical Format for Years 1790 to Present," http://www.measuringworth.org/usgdp/.

Table 1.2   U.S. financial panics that led to recessions, 1837–2008

Unlike the British government in the mid 1760s, the U.S. government did not actively exacerbate panics. Outright rebellion was thereby avoided, but as table 1.2 shows, those episodes had significant political repercussions. J. P. Morgan's strenuous efforts to stymie panic with private means in 1907 caused considerable consternation. He was only partially successful, yet the mere attempt portended power that many Americans believed no individual should hold. They began to see the virtues of government involvement in macroeconomic management. The Federal Reserve System (a.k.a. the Fed), the nation's first central bank since the demise of the (second) Bank of the United States, was the result.[38]

Ironically given its origins, the early Fed was not a potent foe of financial panics. It sat idly by during the Panic of 1919, and by most accounts it exacerbated the Great Depression and helped to bring on the so-called Roosevelt Recession of 1937–38 by unexpectedly raising banks' reserve requirements three times.[39] It was not rigorously tested again until the 1970s, when it allowed inflation to severely disrupt the functioning of numerous financial institutions, especially life insurers and mortgage banks. Under the long reigns of Paul Volcker (1979–87) and Alan Greenspan (1987–2006), however, the Fed began to take on a mythical glow. Volcker slayed inflation, while Greenspan prevented the stock market crash of 1987 from leading to recession, brokered a private bailout of Long-Term Capital Management in 1998, and kept Russian and Southeast Asian financial explosions from negatively impacting the U.S. economy. A few years later, he saw the financial system through the Y2K conversion, ensured that the bursting of the dot-com bubble would lead to only a short and mild recession, and steadied the financial system after the terrorist attacks in September 2001. In so doing, however, Greenspan helped lay the foundations for the crises of 2007 and 2008.[40]

Contrary to Hamilton nee Bagehot's Rule, the Fed under Greenspan fought financial panics by cutting the main interest rates under its control (the discount rate at which the Fed itself made loans to member banks and the federal funds rate at which banks lent to each other overnight). That deviation had two major effects. First, it created moral hazard by signaling to financiers that if they ran into trouble the Fed would help them out of it, and cheaply at that. Second, its easy-money policies kept major market interest rates low for several years. From over 8% in 2000, rates on 30-year mortgages dropped to just over 5% in late 2003. Cheap financing meant that people could afford to pay more for houses, making it one of the leading causes of the real estate bubble that developed in the wake of the 2001 recession.[41]

A major increase in the supply of mortgages was an important contributor too, and came independently of the Fed's policies. Since the Great Depression, the federal government has played a major role in American mortgage markets as a guarantor of loan repayments and as a major supporter of securitization, the packaging of mortgages for resale to investors. Mortgage lending is inherently difficult, especially for banks that rely on deposits and other short-term loans. If interest rates increase, as they did in the 1970s due to inflation, mortgage lenders quickly get into trouble because they have to pay more for their funds (short-term deposits and loans) than they earn on their long-term mortgages. If interest rates decrease, borrowers refinance into lower interest rate loans, usually without penalty, and lenders lose again. Lenders also lose if they lend too much in economically hard-hit geographical areas, like Texas after the 1970s oil boom, New England in the late 1980s, or Manhattan, Southern California, and southern Florida in the first decade of the twenty-first century.

One way for lenders to reduce those risks is to place hundreds, thousands, even tens of thousands of mortgages together into bonds, called mortgage-backed securities (MBSs), and sell them to institutional investors with longer time horizons, like life insurers and pension funds. With the proceeds from the MBS sales, banks can lend again and again, as often as needed to meet demand, and earn nice profits without bearing interest rate or credit risk. For those reasons, mortgage securitization schemes were tried six times in the United States between the Civil War and World War II. All of them failed because mortgage originators received their commissions at closing, which rewarded them for authorizing loans to anyone and everyone rather than for carefully screening good risks from bad. In Europe, by contrast, government-sponsored mortgage securitization had succeeded in making mortgages more affordable and more available.[42]

Disgusted with the massive mortgage foreclosures that plagued Depression-era America, the federal government in 1938 established an agency, the Federal National Mortgage Association (a.k.a. Fannie Mae), dedicated to developing the nation's securitized mortgage markets. That may have been good policy, but in 1968 the government made a major blunder by privatizing Fannie Mae in order to remove it from the federal budget. In 1970, the government created a competitor named the Federal Home Mortgage Corporation (a.k.a. Freddie Mac). Although private shareholders owned and controlled both companies, the government implicitly guaranteed their debt, allowing them to borrow more cheaply than anyone else in the market except the U.S. Treasury. Unsurprisingly, the companies took on enormous amounts of risk by leveraging themselves up to 30 to 1. Instead of stopping the madness occurring in the subprime market, they exacerbated it.[43]

Fannie and Freddie were not the only large financial institutions earning almost riskless profits. After the bankruptcy of Continental Illinois in 1984 forced a government rescue, federal financial regulators made it clear that they believed the nation's largest banks were "too big to fail" (TBTF).[44] In other words, the government promised to step in to save banks if their failure threatened to spread to other parts of the financial system and thereby endanger macroeconomic stability (output, employment, inflation, and so forth). Deregulation led to the extension of the concept to a variety of bank and non-bank financial institutions thought to be too big or too complex to fail.[45] Even more than deposit insurance, which banks have to pay for (though they likely do not pay enough),[46] TBTF creates moral hazard, encouraging big companies and their creditors to earn enormous profits on equally enormous risks ultimately covered by taxpayers.[47]

Unsurprisingly, large financial institutions strove to become and remain behemoths if for no other reason than to *force* the government to come to their rescue in times of trouble.[48] "Those of us who made the decision" to bail out Continental Illinois, noted FDIC director Irvine Sprague, "were convinced we had no other choice.... We were afraid not to.... We believed the very fabric of our banking system was at stake."[49] Political considerations rather than solid science appear to dictate which companies receive TBTF treatment, which at a minimum protects uninsured creditors from loss.[50]

Three other major hybrid failures also contributed to the crises of 2007 and 2008: executive compensation, rating agencies, and tax incentives. Regulators have long since wrestled the right to monitor executives away from stockholders by making it expensive for large institutional investors to throw their weight around in boardrooms, proxy fights, and the like. Those same regulators, however, failed to understand that the structure of executive compensation is absolutely crucial to long-term company performance. Executives rewarded with stock options will run the stock price up and cash in, even if their actions ensure that the price will tumble soon after. Bonuses paid before profits are actually accrued induce managers to expand lines of business, like subprime mortgages, that are profitable in the short term but doomed to fail in the long run. When the true nature of the business reveals itself years later, the manager may lose his job, but he will already have made millions. Some mutual life insurance companies understand this and defer executive compensation for years and even decades. Investment banking partnerships used to do the same thing, for their own self-preservation. When they went public, however, managerial incentives changed, but regulators did not catch on. In 2008, all the major investment banks failed, merged, or became commercial banks—and cost taxpayers billions.[51]

The credit-rating agencies are also hybrid failures. From their emergence in the late nineteenth century until the third quarter of the twentieth century, the agencies rated the quality of bonds and other securities and sold the ratings to investors. The advent of cheap photocopying, however, hurt their business model by allowing shady entrepreneurs to inexpensively copy and resell the bond books to investors at prices far below what the agencies, which expended large sums to create the ratings, could afford to offer. The agencies countered by charging the securities issuers for ratings. Regulators not only allowed this, they encouraged it by mandating that most types of institutional investors could invest only in investment-grade securities as defined by Moody's, Standard and Poor's, and a small handful of other agencies. To curry favor with issuers, the rating agencies naturally engaged in grade inflation. Many investors knew that the agencies were not providing accurate ratings but continued to use them anyway because regulators forced them to or because they believed that the agencies' exemption from disclosure laws like Regulation FD (full disclosure) provided them with inside information. "The market perceives the rating agencies to be doing much more than they actually do," argues institutional investor David Einhorn.[52] That, of course, created the false sense of security that helped fuel the asset bubble underlying the crisis.[53]

Demand for subprime mortgages was undeniably strong, but even here a seeming market failure—millions of people borrowing more than they rationally should have—was actually hybrid in nature. Americans strive for homeownership partly for its own sake, to partake of any price appreciation, to live free of a landlord's whims, and to be able to improve or divide the property as they see fit. But they also own because the government rewards them for doing so via a large number of "affordable housing" initiatives. Since 1977, for example, the Community Reinvestment Act has forced banks to lend to low-income borrowers or forgo regulatory approval for mergers or new activities. In 1993, the government stepped up that demand by urging banks to lower their standards for poorer borrowers. Under clear and persistent pressure, banks eventually complied, with NINJA (no income, no job or assets), liar's (no documentation), and other questionable classes of loans.

The biggest and hoariest affordable housing initiative of all is the mortgage interest tax deduction. Due to that deduction, which has grown in importance as marginal income rates and nominal incomes have risen, Americans tend to stay heavily mortgaged rather than building equity in their homes as they did in the nineteenth century and first half of the twentieth. Favorable tax treatment of retirement savings made the situation even worse because Americans correctly calculated that they were better off putting x percent of their pre-tax pay into a retirement account, getting an x percent match from their employer, and earning a modest investment return than paying down the principal on their mortgage and reducing their interest payment deduction.[54]

Preventing a repeat of 2007–8 will require ending one or more of the hybrid failures that caused the crisis. The government could start by eliminating tax incentives to invest in the stock market instead of in homes. It could also encourage companies to devise deferred compensation structures, especially for executives in long-term financial businesses. Fannie and Freddie, already in conservatorship, should be wound down completely or nationalized so that socialized risks will also lead to socialized profits.[55] Similarly, the government should tax companies that are too big or complex to fail. The precise form the tax should take raises difficult technical issues that cannot be addressed here, but the basic concept is sound. Systemic disturbances caused by the failure of big financial institutions are negative externalities as surely as carbon emissions are.[56] A variety of other plausible reforms have also been proffered.[57]

It is important to point out, however, that no set of reforms can prevent all future financial crises, which take many forms. As long as scarcity, asymmetric information, uncertainty, and risk plague humanity, crises are bound to recur.[58] When weighing their response options, policymakers should consider the tradeoff between short-term macroeconomic stabilization and the long-term damage created by hybrid failures, increased moral hazard, and diminished government credibility. With that in mind, government should rarely resort to bailouts, and when it does it should prefer Hamilton's Rule and other bailouts that do not socialize risk while privatizing profit.[59]

NOTES

1   Peter L. Bernstein, *Against the Gods: The Remarkable Story of Risk* (New York: Wiley and Sons, 1996), 1.

2   Examples of this are too numerous to list. Consider, as an example, the response of bankers to the FDIC's request that they join in on the bailout of Continental Illinois: "The bankers said they wanted to be in on any deal, but they did not want to lose any money. They kept asking for guarantees. They wanted it to look as if they were putting money in but, at the same time, wanted to be absolutely sure they were not risking anything." Irvine H. Sprague, *Bailout: An Insider's Account of Bank Failures and Rescues* (New York: Basic Books, 1986), 158.

3   David Moss, *When All Else Fails: Government as the Ultimate Risk Manager* (Cambridge, MA: Harvard University Press, 2002).

4   This is the premise of the Social Science Research Council series on the Privatization of Risk, of which this volume is a part. See Jacob S. Hacker, ed., *Health at Risk: America's Ailing Health System — and How to Heal It* (New York: Columbia University Press/SSRC, 2008); Andrew Lakoff, ed., *Disaster and the Politics of Intervention* (New York: Columbia University Press/SSRC, forthcoming); Donald W. Light, ed., *The Risks of Prescription Drugs* (New York: Columbia University Press/SSRC, forthcoming); Katherine S. Newman, ed., *Laid Off, Laid Low: Political and Economic Consequences of Employment Insecurity* (New York: Columbia University Press/SSRC, 2008); and Mitchell A. Orenstein, ed., *Pensions, Social Security, and the Privatization of Risk* (New York: Columbia University Press/SSRC, 2009).

5   International bailouts will not be considered here. For a good recent survey of them, see Nouriel Roubini and Brad Setser, *Bailouts or Bail-ins? Responding to Financial Crises in Emerging Economies* (Washington, DC: Council on Foreign Relations, 2004).

6   Anthony Santomero and Paul Hoffman, "Problem Bank Resolution: Evaluating the Options," in *International Banking Crises: Large-Scale Failures, Massive Government Interventions*, ed. Benton E. Gup (Westport, CT: Quorum Books, 1999), 250.

7   Robert E. Wright and George Smith, *Mutually Beneficial: The Guardian and Life Insurance in America* (New York: New York University Press, 2004), 80, 318, 329.

8   Joe Peek and James A. Wilcox, "The Fall and Rise of Banking Safety Net Subsidies," in *Too Big to Fail: Policies and Practices in Government Bailouts*, ed. Benton E. Gup (Westport, CT: Praeger, 2004), 169–93.

9   J. Patrick Raines, J. Ashley McLeod, and Charles G. Leathers, "Theories of Stock Prices and the Greenspan-Bernanke Doctrine on Stock Market Bubbles," *Journal of Post Keynesian Economics* 29, no. 3 (May 2007): 393–408.

10   Benton E. Gup and Philip Bartholomew, "The Decision to Fail Banks: A Global View," in *International Banking Crises: Large-Scale Failures, Massive Government Interventions*, ed. Benton E. Gup (Westport, CT: Quorum Books, 1999), 215.

11   Santomero and Hoffman, "Problem Bank Resolution," 254–56.

12   Benton E. Gup, "What Does Too Big to Fail Mean?" in *Too Big to Fail: Policies and Practices in Government Bailouts*, ed. Benton E. Gup (Westport, CT: Praeger, 2004), 33–34.

13   Sprague, *Bailout*, 251, 256.

14   Sprague, *Bailout*, xi, 3.

15   For additional proposals to limit moral hazard, see Robert Hetzel, "Government Intervention in Financial Markets: Stabilizing or Destabilizing?" (working paper, Federal Reserve Bank of Richmond, February 12, 2009).

16   William J. Baumol, Robert E. Litan, and Carl J. Schramm, *Good Capitalism, Bad Capitalism, and the Economics of Growth and Prosperity* (New Haven, CT: Yale University Press, 2007), 231.

17   David Schramm, "Individual and Social Costs of Divorce in Utah," *Journal of Family and Economic Issues* 27, no. 1 (Spring 2006): 133–51.

18   Barry B. LePatner, Timothy C. Jacobson, and Robert E. Wright, *Broken Buildings, Busted Budgets: How to Fix America's Trillion-Dollar Construction Industry* (Chicago: University of Chicago Press, 2007); and Robert E. Wright, *Fubarnomics* (Buffalo, NY: Prometheus, forthcoming).

19   Lawrence J. White, "The Residential Real Estate Brokerage Industry: What Would More Vigorous Competition Look Like?" *Real Estate Law Journal* 34 (Summer 2006): 22–42.

20   Joseph W. Eaton and David J. Eaton, *The American Title Insurance Industry: How a Cartel Fleeces the American Consumer* (New York: New York University Press, 2007).

21   Anne Matthews, *Bright College Years: Inside the American Campus Today* (Chicago: University of Chicago Press, 1997); Kenneth Lasson, *Trembling in the Ivory Tower: Excesses in the Pursuit of Truth and Tenure* (New York: Bancroft Press, 2003); Peter

Smith, *The Quiet Crisis: How Higher Education is Failing America* (New York: Anker Publishing Company, 2004); and Robert E. Wright, *Higher Education and the Common Weal: Protecting Economic Growth and Political Stability with Professional Partnerships* (Hyderabad, India: ICFAI, 2009).

22   Mancur Olson, *The Rise and Decline of Nations: Economic Growth, Stagflation, and Social Rigidities* (New Haven, CT: Yale University Press, 1982).

23   John R. Wilke, "How Lawmaker Rebuilt Hometown on Earmarks," *Wall Street Journal*, October 30, 2007.

24   Shailagh Murray, "For a Senate Foe of Pork Barrel Spending, Two Bridges Too Far," *Washington Post*, October 21, 2005.

25   Gordon Tullock, Arthur Seldon, and Gordon L. Brady, *Government Failure: A Primer in Public Choice* (Washington, DC: Cato Institute, 2002); and Clifford Winston, *Government Failure vs. Market Failure: Microeconomics Policy Research and Government Performance* (Washington, DC: AEI-Brookings Joint Center for Regulatory Studies, 2006).

26   Charles Wolf Jr., *Markets or Governments: Choosing Between Imperfect Alternatives*, 2nd ed. (Cambridge, MA: MIT Press, 1993).

27   Milton Friedman and Rose Friedman, *Free to Choose: A Personal Statement* (New York: Harcourt Brace Jovanovich, 1980).

28   Robert E. Wright, "On the Economic Efficiency of Organizations: Toward a Solution of the Efficient Government Enterprise Paradox," *Essays in Economic and Business History* 25 (April 2007): 143–54.

29   Price Fishback et al., *Government and the American Economy: A New History* (Chicago: Chicago University Press, 2007), 403, 462; Amity Shlaes, *The Forgotten Man: A New History of the Great Depression* (New York: HarperCollins, 2007); and Tullock, Seldon, and Brady, *Government Failure*, 61.

30   Except where otherwise noted, this section is based upon Robert E. Wright and Vincenzo Quadrini, *Money and Banking* (Nyack, NY: Flat World Knowledge, 2009), which is available at: http://www.flatworldknowledge.com/printed-book/1634.

31   Bruce H. Mann, *Republic of Debtors: Bankruptcy in the Age of American Independence* (Cambridge, MA: Harvard University Press, 2003).

32   The three incentives examples (ice cream, debt collection bonuses, and stock options) introduced here are described in Wright, "On the Economic Efficiency."

33   Eugene White, *Crashes and Panics: The Lessons from History* (New York: Dow Jones–Irwin, 1990); and Standard and Poor's, "S&P/Case-Shiller Home Price Indices:

Historical Home Price Values," http://www2.standardandpoors.com/portal/site/
sp/en/us/page.topic/indices_csmahp/2,3,4,0,0,0,0,0,0,0,0,0,0,0,0,0.html.

34   Mike Flynn, "Anatomy of a Breakdown: Concerted Government Policy Helped
     Trigger the Financial Meltdown—And Will Almost Certainly Extend It," *Reason*,
     January 2009: 28–34.

35   Tim Arango, "The Housing-Bubble and the American Revolution," *New York
     Times*, November 29, 2008.

36   Richard Sylla, Robert E. Wright, and David J. Cowen, "Alexander Hamilton, Cen-
     tral Banker: Crisis Management During the U.S. Financial Panic of 1792," *Busi-
     ness History Review* 83, no. 1 (Spring 2009): 61–86; and Robert E. Wright, *One
     Nation Under Debt: Hamilton, Jefferson, and the History of What We Owe* (New York:
     McGraw-Hill, 2008), 157–60.

37   Burton W. Folsom Jr., *The Myth of the Robber Barons: A New Look at the Rise of Big
     Business in America*, 5th ed. (Herndon, VA: Young America's Foundation, 2007).

38   Robert F. Bruner and Sean D. Carr, *The Panic of 1907: Lessons Learned from the
     Market's Perfect Storm* (Hoboken, NJ: Wiley & Sons, 2007).

39   This statement is not meant to take a position in the large, highly politicized debate
     over the efficacy of the New Deal.

40   Robert L. Hetzel, *The Monetary Policy of the Federal Reserve: A History* (New York:
     Cambridge University Press, 2008); and Stephen H. Axilrod, *Inside the Fed: Mone-
     tary Policy and Its Management, Martin Through Greenspan to Bernanke* (Cambridge,
     MA: MIT Press, 2009).

41   William A. Fleckenstein and Frederick Sheehan, *Greenspan's Bubbles: The Age of
     Ignorance at the Federal Reserve* (New York: McGraw-Hill, 2008).

42   Kenneth Snowden, "Mortgage Securitization in the United States: Twentieth Cen-
     tury Developments in Historical Perspective," in *Anglo-American Financial Systems:
     Institutions and Markets in the Twentieth Century*, ed. Michael D. Bordo and Richard
     Sylla (Burr Ridge, IL: Irwin Professional Publishing, 1995), 261–98.

43   Rob Alford, "What Are the Origins of Freddie Mac and Fannie Mae?" *History News
     Network*, December 8, 2003.

44   Continental Illinois was the trigger; TBTF doctrine ultimately stemmed from Sec-
     tion 13(c)(4)(A) of the FDIC Act of 1950, the so-called essentiality doctrine, which
     empowered the bailout of any bank that the FDIC deemed in danger of failing and
     "essential to provide adequate banking service in its community," a vague clause
     the FDIC has interpreted to mean any bank the failure of which presents "a clear

and present danger to the nation's financial system." Sprague, *Bailout*, 27–29, 259; and Gary H. Stern and Ron J. Feldman, *Too Big to Fail: The Hazards of Bank Bailouts* (Washington, DC: Brookings Institution Press, 2004), viii–ix.

45 Stern and Feldman, *Too Big to Fail*, 60–79; and Gup, "What Does Too Big," 29–48.

46 Peek and Wilcox, "The Fall and Rise," 169–93.

47 Sprague, *Bailout*, 260–64; and Stern and Feldman, *Too Big to Fail*, 1–2.

48 Marcelo Dabos, "Too Big to Fail in the Banking Industry: A Survey," in *Too Big to Fail: Policies and Practices in Government Bailouts*, ed. Benton E. Gup (Westport, CT: Praeger, 2004), 141.

49 Sprague, *Bailout*, xi, 4, 9–10, 149–230, 244, 250.

50 Stern and Feldman, *Too Big to Fail*, xi–xii, 5.

51 Vincent P. Carosso, *Investment Banking in America: A History* (Cambridge, MA: Harvard University Press, 1970); Lisa Endlich, *Goldman Sachs: The Culture of Success* (New York: Simon & Schuster, 1999); Wright and Smith, *Mutually Beneficial*, 385–90; and Viral V. Acharya and Matthew Richardson, eds., *Restoring Financial Stability: How to Repair a Failed System* (Hoboken, NJ: Wiley, 2009).

52 David Einhorn, "Private Profits and Socialized Risk" (speech given at Spring 2008 Grant's Conference, New York, April 8, 2008), http://www.grantspub.com/UserFiles/File/Einhorn_Grants_Conference_04-08-2008.pdf.

53 Lawrence J. White, "The Credit-Rating Agencies' Legally Protected Monopoly," *Critical Review: A Journal of Politics and Society* 21, no. 1 (2009); and *Economist*, "The Wages of Sin: The Fed is Perpetuating a Discredited Oligopoly," April 25, 2009, 80.

54 Roger Lowenstein, "Who Needs the Mortgage-Interest Deduction?" *New York Times*, March 5, 2006; and Tullock, Seldon, and Brady, *Government Failure*, 63–64.

55 Government agencies need not be inefficient. As a first approximation, an organization's efficiency is a function of the structure of the market in which it operates and its internal incentive structure. Organizations operating in competitive markets that have compatible internal incentive structures will be efficient, while those in monopoly markets with weak internal incentives will not, regardless of their ownership structures. Wright, "On the Economic Efficiency," 143–54.

56 Sprague, *Bailout*, 249–50; Acharya and Richardson, *Restoring Financial Stability*; and Stern and Feldman, *Too Big to Fail*, 190–92.

57 Dabos, "Too Big to Fail," 141–51.

58 Sprague, *Bailout*, 231–34.

59 Hamilton/Bagehot's Rule was promulgated when a specie standard (silver and/ or gold) was in place. Under that system, the domestic money supply was determined by international markets. Today, the central bank (the Federal Reserve in the United States) determines the domestic money supply. While bailing out firms by lending on good collateral at a penalty rate, central banks today also need to ensure that money supply growth continues at an appropriate rate. If necessary, a central bank can do so by using standard instruments, such as purchasing risk-free government bonds in the open market, or by distributing new money directly to taxpayers.

CHAPTER TWO

Financial Crises and Government Responses: Lessons Learned

BENTON E. GUP

Governments respond to real and perceived threats to the economic stability of their countries using a variety of threat-dependent methods aimed first at eliminating or mitigating the threat and secondarily at promoting financial stability and economic growth. Only then do governments address causal issues, and in a fashion that may or may not reduce the chances of future crises. The U.S. government's responses to the financial and economic crisis of 2007 to 2009 have been no exception. The government has attempted to minimize the crisis's considerable costs, which include lost income and employment and a rapidly augmenting national debt. In so doing, however, the government may be laying the foundation for yet another crisis. It is hoped that once the current crisis subsides, the government will examine its causes and take effective measures to decrease the likelihood of recurrence.

To that end, this chapter examines the specific causes of the current crisis in the context of recent crises worldwide ("Causes"), details the U.S. government's responses to financial crises ("Reactions"), and concludes that the government needs to take a more proactive role in preventing future crises ("Conclusions").

CAUSES

Key players in financial crises include borrowers, lenders, and regulators. Government policies intended to stimulate economic growth can have unintended consequences, including the initiation of an asset bubble or cyclical expansion (boom). For example, low interest rates, policies encouraging home ownership, and government-sponsored enterprises (or GSEs, like "Fannie Mae" and "Freddie Mac") facilitated the recent real estate boom. Conventional mortgage rates on new homes peaked at 14.49% in 1982 and subsequently declined to just 5.8% in 2003.[1] Lending standards loosened considerably too. Unfortunately, many of the mortgages could only be maintained when the economy was robust and housing prices were rising. When rising energy prices and other factors resulted in slower economic growth, housing prices and incomes began to decline, inducing many borrowers to default.

That is problematic because if a sufficiently large number of borrowers default, some banks will fail. If the defaults occur en masse, a large number of banks will fail. Thus far, there have been enough bank failures to negatively affect the capital markets and the outlook of businesses, which have responded by decreasing employment. That has increased defaults, endangering yet more banks and further clouding the economic horizon. Increased U.S. exports ameliorated the situation somewhat until the financial crisis spread abroad in a process called contagion. Securitized real estate loans (called mortgage-backed securities, or MBSs, and collateralized debt obligations, or CDOs) that originated in the United States soon infected the European and Asian financial institutions that acquired them during the boom. During the bust, rising levels of default by American homeowners caused banking problems in the United Kingdom, Germany, Japan, and elsewhere.

The current crisis is not the first to stem from the real estate sector. Between 1980 and 1996, more than 130 of the International Monetary Fund's 181 members experienced significant banking sector problems or crises.[2] Fluctuations in real estate conditions were specifically connected to banking problems in Finland, France, Japan, Malaysia, Norway, Spain, Sweden, the United States, Venezuela, and elsewhere. In a World Bank study of bank restructuring during the 1980s, real estate losses were associated with banking problems in Argentina, Chile, Columbia, Ghana, Malaysia, Spain, the United States, and Yugoslavia.[3] A Federal Deposit

Insurance Corporation (FDIC) study concluded that booms and busts in commercial real estate markets were the main causes of losses at failed and surviving banks during the U.S. banking crises in the 1980s and early 1990s.[4] Former FDIC chairman William Seidman concurred, noting that "everywhere from Finland to Sweden to England to the United States to Japan to Australia, excessive real estate loans created the core of the banking problem."[5] Studies of individual bank failures in the G-10 countries also identified real estate loans as contributing to more bank failures than any other single category of loans.[6] Nations where problem real estate loans could be linked to individual bank failures included Canada, France, Japan, the Netherlands, and the United States. Losses in real estate loans and other long-term loans also played an important role in the 1997–98 financial crises in Southeast Asia.

Real estate mortgages, like other types of loans, are especially problematic when they employ high degrees of financial leverage, or in other words when borrowers have little equity in the investment. Statistical studies corroborate what common sense suggests, that loan-to-value ratios (size of the mortgage divided by the market value of the property) are significant determinants of mortgage loan default rates.[7] In addition, other factors constant, borrowers with low credit ratings are more likely to default than those with high credit ratings. Finally, borrowers are more likely to default when the market value of the real estate falls below the amount they owe to the lender, a major problem when real estate prices decrease across the board.

Of course not all financial crises begin with bad loans, which are a type of credit risk, or "the risk that one party to a financial contract will fail to discharge an obligation and thus cause the other party to incur a financial loss."[8] Losses can also stem from market risk, or "the risk of losses on financial instruments arising from changes in market prices," and liquidity risk, or "the risk that assets may not be readily available to meet a demand for cash."[9] Consider, for example, the case of Long-Term Capital Management (LTCM) of Greenwich, Connecticut, once a successful hedge fund. Partners of the firm included Nobel laureates Merton Miller and Myron Scholes, former Federal Reserve vice chairman David W. Mullins Jr., and former Salomon Inc. trader John W. Meriwether, who together developed a quantitative model of trading that generated substantial profits so long as its underlying assumptions remained realistic.

In spite of their collective wisdom and insights, LTCM's partners did not foresee the impact of global market turmoil on financial markets, so the large bets they placed on credit spreads and equity derivatives resulted in huge losses that the highly leveraged fund ($50 of assets for every $1 of equity) could not absorb. (Banks are considered highly leveraged at 12.5 to 1, and corporations when leveraged at 3 to 1.) In other words, LTCM succumbed to market and liquidity, rather than credit, risk. LTCM's creditors, though, faced a major credit risk, the hedge fund's inability to repay its loans.

Fearful that the rapid unwinding of LTCM's multibillion-dollar positions would result in large losses for banks and brokers who had extended the hedge fund credit, the Federal Reserve Bank of New York brokered a private bailout by pressuring lenders to extend the troubled hedge fund a lifeline. A consortium of commercial and investment banks, including Goldman Sachs, Merrill Lynch, Morgan Stanley Dean Witter, Travelers Group, and UBS Securities, responded with a $3.5 billion loan package.[10] Some banks lost money on the transaction. UBS, then the world's largest bank, took a $700 million write down, and Germany's Dresdner Bank lost $143 million. Those losses, however, were offset by the large profits those banks made from the hedge fund in previous years.

Excessive leverage and risks and flawed quantitative models also lie at the root of the problems recently experienced by insurance giant AIG. On behalf of AIG, Yale finance professor Gary Gorton developed quantitative models based on historical data to predict the likelihood of default of credit-default swaps (CDSs), a type of derivative designed to allow financial institutions to hedge counterparty default risk.[11] The models, on which AIG depended for assessing CDS deals, worked well at first, but they did not attempt to measure the risk of future collateral calls, write downs, or other unusual variables that increased in importance as the subprime crisis intensified. Ultimately, reliance on the models devastated AIG's finances. The lesson here appears to be that while quantitative models can be useful and should be employed to assess risks, they have limits that must be clearly understood before excessive reliance is placed upon them.

Commercial banks, by contrast, typically succumb to credit and/or interest rate risk. (Fraud can also play a role but is beyond the scope of this chapter.)[12] Privately owned banks attempt to maximize shareholder wealth by making profitable loans (maximizing spreads between deposits and other borrowings and loans and minimizing expenses) and by increasing leverage (increasing loan portfolios and assets while maintaining the same base of equity). Interest income from loans is the primary source of bank income, so increasing profits often entails making higher risk loans with higher rates of interest. Unsurprisingly, bad loans are the primary reason for bank failures. If the number of non-performing loans is sufficiently large, the bank's capital can be eroded to the point that regulators or depositors and other creditors shutter the institution.

Consider the balance sheet of the hypothetical bank shown in table 2.1, panel A. The bank's sole asset is a single loan funded by deposits and stockholder equity. The ratio of equity (E) capital to risk-assets (A) is 10% (E/A = 10/100), sufficiently large for the bank to be considered "well-capitalized" by regulators. In addition, the bank is very profitable, with a return on assets (ROA) of 2.88% (about 1% ROA is considered good for commercial banks in the United States). Nevertheless, the bank's stakeholders want it to grow so that they garner higher returns on their investments, employees get larger salaries, communities can grow, and so forth.

In order to grow, the bank raises an additional $20 million in deposits and invests them in two loans of $10 million each (table 2.1, panel B).[13] No additional loan-loss reserves are required. ROA is now 2.73% and E/A is 8.33%, so the bank is "adequately capitalized" in the eyes of regulators. In the next period (table 2.1, panel C), one of the $10 million loans defaults for some reason. Because the $10 million default exceeds the loan-loss reserve by $8 million, the difference must be deducted from stockholder equity, leaving only $2 million. Suddenly, the bank has an E/A of only 1.79% and is "critically undercapitalized," requiring regulators to fail it or shut it down. Note that the loan default itself did not cause the bank's demise — the default combined with the bank's high degree of leverage did. It simply did not have sufficient capital to cover the loss.

Leverage also affects borrowers' decisions. Suppose that a home buyer purchases a $500,000 house by borrowing 100% of its value. If the house price declines any significant amount, say 15% to $425,000, the borrower is likely to default on the loan. However, if the borrower had put $100,000 equity into the home, borrowing only 80% of the

Panel A

ASSETS ($ MILLIONS)		LIABILITIES	
Loan	$102 @ 9%	Deposits	$90 @ 7%
Loan loss reserve	− 2		
Net loans	$100		
		Stockholders' equity	$10
Totals	$100		$100

NET INCOME	$9.18 − 6.30 = $2.88
RETURN ON ASSETS (ROA)	$2.88 / 100 = 2.88%
EQUITY/ASSETS (E/A)	$10 / 100 = 10% *well capitalized*

Panel B

ASSETS ($ MILLIONS)		LIABILITIES	
Loan	$102 @ 9%	Deposits	$110 @ 7%
Loan	10 @ 9%		
Loan	10 @ 9%		
Loan loss reserve	− 2		
Net loans	$120		
		Stockholders' equity	$10
Totals	$120		$120

NET INCOME	$10.98 − 7.70 = $3.28
RETURN ON ASSETS (ROA)	$3.28 / 120 = 2.73%
EQUITY/ASSETS (E/A)	$10 / 120 = 8.33% *adequately capitalized*

Panel C

ASSETS ($ MILLIONS)		LIABILITIES	
Loan	$102 @ 9%	Deposits	$110 @ 7%
Loan	10 @ 9%		
Loan default	− 10		
Loan loss reserve	2		
Net loans	$112		
		Stockholders' equity	$2
Totals	$112		$112

Defaulted loan $10, exceed loan loss reserve by $8, which is deducted from stockholders' equity.

NET INCOME	$10.08 − 7.70 = $2.38
RETURN ON ASSETS (ROA)	$2.88 / 112 = 2.13%
EQUITY/ASSETS (E/A)	$2 / 112 = 1.79% *critically undercapitalized*
	= BANK FAILURE

Table 2.1 Bank growth and losses (credit risk) [Source: Author.]

purchase price, the borrower would be much less likely to default, all other factors equal, because he or she would still have $25,000 of equity in the house.

When large numbers of highly leveraged borrowers default on loans made by numerous highly leveraged banks, the compounding effect results in a banking crisis. Securitization, the packaging and selling of otherwise unmarketable loans to other financial institutions and investors, amplified leverage by increasing adverse selection, a form of asymmetric information (see chapter 1 for a description of asymmetric information). Sellers of securitized loans (originators like brokers and investment banks) have better information about the quality of the borrowers than the buyers do, allowing them to offload their riskiest mortgages at higher prices and quantities than they otherwise could. Because mortgage originators did not retain an equity (potential loss) position in the securitization process and received full compensation upon closing or selling a mortgage, they suffered no losses when the loans they sold defaulted. That created a moral hazard problem because the system basically provided them with incentives to maximize the quantity and minimize the quality of mortgage deals. Most of the predatory lending practices observed during the bubble — techniques that cajoled home purchasers to borrow more than they could afford — were the result of the unregulated incentive structure that encouraged such behaviors.

Moreover, the securitized assets lacked transparency, and credit-rating agencies like Moody's and Standard and Poor's misjudged their quality. To assign credit ratings, the agencies depend on quantitative models like those described above. Unfortunately, they did not perform well rating mortgage-backed securities (MBSs), collateralized debt obligations (CDOs), and other complex derivatives when the economic conditions changed dramatically. Thus, many purchasers of securitized subprime loans did not realize the high level of risk they were assuming. Many financial institutions that acquired MBSs also bought credit-default swaps (CDSs), a form of insurance that they thought would reduce the risk of holding the mortgages. As previously noted, CDS issuers like AIG were unable to provide the protection they promised, further contributing to the losses associated with securitized subprime loans. It is important to note, however, that not all securitized loan products are tainted or misused. When used properly, securitization is a useful tool. Moral hazard can be greatly reduced by requiring originators and investment banks to retain a portion of (take equity positions in) the securitized loans and by making the instruments more transparent.

Interest rate risk, the risk to earnings or capital as a result of changes in interest rates, can also cripple banks. With respect to an entire bank, it is the negative effect on net interest income from a mismatch between the dollar amounts of interest rate–sensitive assets and interest rate–sensitive liabilities. Interest rate risk also relates to the market value of bank assets, including mortgage loans. If market interest rates increase, the value of fixed-income assets, like bonds and fixed-rate mortgages, that are held for sale or investment declines, while the value of liabilities remains unchanged, resulting in a loss of equity capital.

In the late 1970s and early 1980s, most savings and loans (S&Ls) were technically insolvent (liabilities > assets) as a result of interest rate risks. The S&Ls borrowed short-term funds and lent them at fixed rates for long-term mortgage loans. When interest rates soared in the late 1970s and early 1980s, their interest expenses exceeded their interest incomes, resulting in large losses. Insolvent firms can operate as long as their cash flow is positive. However, large numbers of S&Ls failed in the 1980s.

Regulatory capital of commercial banks in the United States is currently based on the book value of their assets and liabilities. That will change when FASB 157 (the Federal Accounting Standards Board [FASB] statement on Fair Value Measurements—a framework for valuing assets and liabilities at their fair value) is adopted as U.S. regulations converge with international accounting standards. Implementation of FASB 157 will have a profound adverse affect on commercial banks that now fund long-term assets that are held for sale or investment with short-term sources of funds when market interest rates increase. Only 975 out of 7,203 insured U.S. commercial banks reported derivatives activities to the Office of the Comptroller of the Currency (OCC) in the second quarter of 2008.[14] That means that most U.S. banks are not using derivatives to hedge against interest rate increases. If interest rates suddenly rise, as they may do if the economy suffers a bout of post-bailout inflation, many banks will become "undercapitalized" under FASB 157 regardless of whether loan payments continue to be paid or the extent to which bank portfolios are well diversified.

Table 2.2 provides the equity capital to asset ratios (E/A) of U.S. banks in selected years between 1896 and 2008. Equity capital, or the book value of assets minus the book value of liabilities, is different than regulatory capital, which can include subordinated debt and some adjust-

DATE	U.S. BANKS (%)	NON-FINANCIAL CORPORATIONS (%)
1896	23.5	
1900	17.9	
1980	5.8	69.1
1988	6.2	
2000	8.5	49.2
2005		35.4
2008	9.67	39.4 (2007)

Source: Author based on Board of Governors of the Federal Reserve System, *All-bank Statistics, United States, 1896–1955* (New York: Arno, 1976); FDIC, *Quarterly Banking Profile: All Institutions Performance Third Quarter 2008* (Washington, DC, 2008), Table III-A; and the 1989, 1998, and 2009 editions of the U.S. Bureau of the Census, *Statistical Abstract of the United States* (Washington, DC).

Table 2.2   U.S. bank equity/asset ratios

ments for off-balance-sheet items. The table also shows that non-financial corporations had E/A ratios that ranged from 35% to 69%, substantially greater than the bank E/A ratios. One reason why banks have lower E/A ratios is that federal and state regulators, like the FDIC, are enjoined by law to take "prompt corrective actions" if a bank's risk-based capital falls below predetermined levels. Risk-based capital ratio refers to the ratio of a percentage of a bank's risk-weighted assets (for example, loans) to its capital accounts. Well-capitalized banks have risk-based capital ratios of 10% or more. Undercapitalized banks have ratios of 6% or less.

Weighting assets by risk category was one of the major initiatives of an international regulator, the Basel Committee on Banking Supervision. Established in 1974, the Basel Committee focused on facilitating and enhancing information sharing and cooperation among bank regulators and developing principles for the supervision of internationally active large banks. Following the large losses incurred by banks that lent to the least developed countries (LDCs) in the late 1970s, it became increasingly concerned about the failure of large banks and cross-border contagion. In particular, it believed that large banks did not have adequate capital in relation to the risks they were assuming. The end result was a uniform (one size fits all) 8% risk-weighted capital requirement that became known as the 1988 Capital Accord, or Basel I.

Although the notion that riskier banks should hold more capital than safe ones was sound, Basel I, in the words of Federal Reserve vice chairman Roger Ferguson, "is too simplistic to address the activities of our most complex banking institutions."[15] Specifically, it is not sufficiently risk sensitive. Under Basel I, bank capital consists of two tiers. Tier 1 includes shareholder equity and retained earnings, and it is 4%. Tier 2 includes additional internal and external funds available to the bank and also is 4%.[16] The 8% "minimum capital is a guidepost.... It was not and is not intended as a level toward which the firms should aim nor as a standard for internal risk management."[17] Unsurprisingly, a large number of failed banks had capital ratios in excess of 8% shortly before failure. According to an FDIC study, 26% of the 1,600 U.S. banks that failed between 1980 and 1994 had CAMEL ratings of 1 or 2 as recently as one year before failure.[18] (Bank regulators use CAMEL—Capital, Asset quality, Management, Earnings, and Liquidity—to evaluate banks on a scale that ranges from a high of 1 to a low of 5.)[19] The study concluded that "bank capital positions are poor predictors of failure several years before the fact."[20]

Getting capital regulations right is important because banking crises are extremely common. Between 1980 and 1996, 133 of the International Monetary Fund's 181 member countries experienced significant banking sector problems.[21] Many of those crises imposed significant real economic costs (decreased employment and output) because bank failures typically come in waves, clustering over time and space following interest rate, exchange rate, asset price, and other shocks. The Basel Committee responded to criticisms and continued banking crises by developing Basel II, which maintains the 8% risk-based capital guideline but attempts to be more risk sensitive than Basel I. Large U.S. banks must be compliant with Basel II capital standards, but it is doubtful that the new guidelines will prove adequate. In 2007, FDIC-insured commercial banks in the United States held 12.23% risk-based capital on average, far in excess of the Basel requirement.[22] The smallest banks (assets of less than $100 million) held 19.84% risk-based capital, while the largest banks (greater than $10 billion) held 11.86%. Banks hold capital in excess of regulatory requirements to cushion them from prompt corrective action by regulators and to take advantage of growth opportunities. In addition, strong earnings and goodwill due to mergers serve to minimize the costs of carrying the extra equity shield.[23]

In addition to its dubious benefit, Basel II may impose significant costs. Analysts have run several Quantitative Impact Studies in order to test various aspects of Basel II. Some believe that Basel II may "lead to an unacceptably large decline in capital for the largest banks" while simultaneously creating "a daunting challenge for the nation's community banks."[24] Others noted that one consequence of forcing banks to increase their capital ratios may be a reduction of lending. For example, U.S. banks trying to meet the Basel I standards contributed to the credit crunch of the early 1990s.[25] In short, Basel II is not likely to prevent future financial crises or to significantly reduce the costs of their resolutions.

REACTIONS

An FDIC study, *History of the Eighties*, argued that "at various times and for various reasons, regulators generally concluded that good public policy required that big banks in trouble be shielded from the full impact of market forces and that their uninsured depositors be protected."[26] The first time that occurred in the United States was in 1984 when bank regulators intervened in the case of Continental Illinois National Bank and Trust Company of Chicago because they feared that its failure might cause a systemic crisis. In the wake of that bailout, comptroller of the currency Todd Conover announced the TBTF (too big to fail) doctrine, which held that the government would not allow any of the nation's eleven largest banks to fail.[27] In the United States, TBTF means that the troubled bank (or other financial institution) may continue to exist, but the stockholders, subordinated debt holders, managers, and some creditors may suffer financial losses. In the case of Continental Illinois, the FDIC assumed a large portion of the bank's bad assets and responsibility for its Federal Reserve loans in exchange for an 80% ownership stake.[28]

Fears that the failure of large, complex financial institutions could wreak havoc on the financial system and ultimately the economy also motivated the 2008 bailouts. In September of that year, the Federal Reserve staved off the bankruptcy of insurance giant AIG by acquiring an 80% stake in the insurer for $85 billion,[29] increased to $150 billion in November.[30] Regulators considered AIG too big to fail because the earlier failure of Lehman Brothers had severely disrupted some financial markets, including the market for CDSs, in which both Lehman and AIG were major players. (AIG underwrote more than $500 billion of the $60 trillion CDS market.)[31] Also in November, the Treasury, Federal Reserve, and FDIC provided Citigroup with "open bank assistance." They invested $20 billion in Citigroup's preferred stock to boost the bank's capital in order to protect it against large losses from loans and securities. With more than two hundred million customers in 106 countries, Citigroup is one of the largest financial institutions in the United States and indeed the world and hence also considered too big to fail. As the crisis worsened, the government aided yet other large banks considered to represent systemic risks.[32]

Government intervention can take many forms depending on its purpose. A wide variety of intervention techniques for banks and other firms have been employed in the long and turbulent history of the United States. Prior to passage of the Banking Act of 1933, national and state banking laws empowered the comptroller of the currency or state bank regulators to assess shareholders of banks to provide additional capital up to the par value of their shares. Those who refused to pay the assessment could have their shares sold by the bank's board of directors.[33] Collection proved costly, so the Banking Act of 1933 eliminated double liability for national banks in favor of federal deposit insurance. States also gradually abandoned super liability provisions. Today, several government agencies are responsible for intervening in the markets to promote financial and economic stability. The FDIC and Federal Reserve can usually handle relatively minor financial market disturbances without further aid or direction, but larger or non-financial crises often require U.S. Department of Treasury and congressional intervention.

The non-performing assets of distressed financial institutions can be removed and taken over by another organization, called a "bad bank," established for that purpose. The bad bank can be privately owned or owned by the FDIC. Similarly, the Competitive Equality Banking Act of 1987 granted the FDIC the power to charter, own, and operate a "bridge bank" as a temporary means for handling large bank failures that pose a risk to the stability of the insurance fund. The FDIC merges the insolvent bank into the bridge bank, which continues operations until the FDIC sells it. The FDIC has several additional intervention techniques at its disposal. With a deposit insurance transfer, the insured and secured deposits of a closed bank can be transferred to another bank that acts as an agent for the FDIC and assumes the responsibility of the payoff.

A payoff of insured depositors of a failed bank occurs when no acquirer has offered a sufficient premium to cover the costs or there is fraud or other claims that make it difficult to determine the losses in order to apply the "cost test." (Under Section 13[c] of the Federal Deposit Insurance Act of 1950, the assistance provided by the FDIC must not exceed the cost of a payoff and liquidation of a failing institution.) In a direct payoff, the FDIC pays off depositors up to the insurance limit, which in 2008 was raised from $100,000 to $250,000.

A "traditional," or "clean bank," purchase and assumption (P&A) refers to the purchase of all or substantially all of a failed bank's assets (cash, securities, some loans, and so forth) and its liabilities. The difference between the values of the acquired assets and the assumed liabilities is covered by a cash payment from the FDIC to the acquirer—an insured bank. The acquiring bank does not have to buy assets that it deems undesirable, and it may return certain assets to the FDIC within a given period of time. In a "whole-bank" transaction, the FDIC sells virtually the entire institution and writes a check to the buyer for the difference between the value of the assumed liabilities and the value of the assets less the premium paid for the franchise value of the institution. The acquirer recapitalizes the newly acquired bank.

Liquidation occurs under Chapter 7 of the Bankruptcy Code. In a receivership, the FDIC retains most or all of a failed bank's assets that are to be liquidated. The decision to liquidate assets or to use a purchase and assumption depends on the outcome of a "cost test."

If the FDIC believes that a troubled institution has not yet become insolvent and is still a viable concern, it may engage in forbearance by not enforcing capital or other supervisory standards. The Garn-St. Germain Act of 1982 provided for the issuance of net worth certificates to qualifying institutions to supplement their capital. Those certificates resulted in the creation of "regulatory capital" that forestalled the enforcement of normal capital standards. The Competitive Equality Banking Act of 1987 also created forbearance opportunities by allowing agricultural banks to amortize losses from the sale or reappraisals of qualified agricultural loans and related properties. The unamortized portion of the losses could be included in the primary capital for purposes of regulatory and supervisory reporting.

As America's central bank, the Federal Reserve's primary responsibility in financial crises is to provide liquidity by acting as a lender of last resort, a role it has played on numerous occasions. Penn Central Railroad, a major issuer of short-term bonds called commercial paper, teetered on the verge of bankruptcy in May 1970 with more than $200 million in commercial paper outstanding. Recognizing the significant negative impact that Penn Central's bankruptcy might have on the commercial paper market, the Federal Reserve Bank of New York provided a direct loan to the firm. After the railroad went bankrupt in June 1970, the Fed (Federal Reserve) lent $575 million to banks and other borrowers. It also suspended interest rate ceilings on deposits (Regulation Q), encouraged money center banks to lend to customers in search of liquidity, and influenced the level of short-term interest rates to aid functioning of the commercial paper market.

In the early 1980s, fears that foreign debt problems in other countries might spill over into the United States and cause massive bank failures and another Great Depression led the Fed to expand the money supply, which grew at a 14.2% annualized rate from the third quarter of 1982 to the second quarter of 1983. A few years later, the Fed faced a similar threat in the domestic market. Monday, October 19, 1987, is called "Black Monday" because the Dow Jones industrial average declined almost 23% on a volume of 604 million shares, at that time the largest daily decline on record. The following day, brokers needed to extend a massive amount of credit to their customers who had margin calls. Fearful that the clearing and settlement system could break down, the Fed announced its readiness to provide liquidity to support the financial system and encouraged banks to lend to solvent securities firms.

The Federal Reserve also regulates bank holding companies, most of which count themselves among the nation's largest depository institutions. Since 1972, the Fed's "source of strength" doctrine has provided that distressed bank affiliates in a holding company can turn to the parent company for financial and managerial aid. The source of strength doctrine became law with the passage of the Financial Institutions Reform, Recovery, and Enforcement Act of 1989 (FIRREA), which requires all commonly controlled banks to be liable for the losses of affiliated banks. The holding company must guarantee the capital restoration plans filed by its undercapitalized affiliates.

The U.S. federal government also reacts to crises, generally in an ad hoc or case-by-case manner, when the FDIC and Federal Reserve cannot provide sufficient aid. In 1932, for example, Congress created the Reconstruction Finance Corporation (RFC) to make secured loans to banks in order to provide them with liquidity to keep them operating as going concerns, a function that the Fed was then unwilling and unable to perform. The tactic failed because the banks invested in low-risk government securities instead of making loans. In 1933, Congress responded by granting the RFC the authority to provide equity capital to the banks in the form of preferred stock. As late as 1951, the RFC held about $93 million in preferred stock in 392 banks.

Bank holidays are a form of forbearance initiated by governments that entails temporarily shuttering the banking system. When Franklin D. Roosevelt was sworn in as president in March 1933, state governments had already declared a bank holiday as a ploy designed to stop bank runs and restore confidence in the banking system. The Ohio thrift crises in March 1986 also resulted in a bank holiday designed to stop depositor runs on banks insured by the Ohio Deposit Guarantee Fund (ODGF), which had been crippled by bank failures. The governor of Ohio closed ODGF-insured institutions for five days until the Ohio legislature agreed to provide assistance for the institutions to convert to federal deposit insurance. The tactic worked; net withdrawals were minimal when the banks reopened.

In the mid 1960s, Lockheed Aircraft Corporation attempted to reduce its dependence on contracts with the Department of Defense (DOD) by reentering the market for commercial jets, investing more than $1.4 billion ($400 million of which came from bank loans) for the development of the L-1011 wide-body passenger jet. The company then suffered a series of setbacks, including before-tax losses of $484 million in contract disputes with the DOD and the commercial failure of the L-1011, which was rolled out when the economy was soft and demand for new airliners slack. Adding to its woes, Rolls-Royce, the supplier of engines for the L-1011, went into receivership in January 1971. The British government would not assure continued delivery of the engines without assurance of continued L-1011 production.

Lockheed's failure would have had major adverse economic consequences in California (a loss of 60,000 jobs) and the nation (a loss of GNP [gross national product] estimated at between $120 and $475 million). It would also have weakened America's national defense capabilities and left only Boeing and McDonnell to compete for aerospace contracts.[34] In August 1971, Congress responded with the Emergency Loan Guarantee Act, the stated purpose of which was to provide emergency loan guarantees for any major business enterprise facing liquidity constraints. The act established an Emergency Loan Guarantee Board under the aegis of the Treasury Department. The board was authorized to grant up to $250 million in loan guarantees and specified some of the conditions of the loans. Lockheed was the first recipient. In return, Lockheed paid loan guarantee and commitment fees to the board, net income of which in fiscal 1972 and 1973 was $5.4 million.[35]

The smallest and least profitable of Detroit's Big Three automakers, Chrysler also received federal loan guarantees when threatened with bankruptcy. The company had higher operating costs than General Motors and Ford, was unsuccessful as a multinational manufacturer, and made poor marketing decisions. In the 1970s, rising energy prices and government safety, pollution, and fuel efficiency regulations added to its problems. In 1978 and 1979 it suffered losses of $218 million and $1.1 billion, respectively. Chrysler was the tenth largest manufacturing company in the United States in 1978 and the seventeenth largest in 1979 when it asked the government for aid. The company argued that without aid it would have to lay off 134,000 workers in Detroit, which was already a high unemployment area. It also claimed that a turnaround was likely if it had time to properly introduce its new K-car, an intermediate-size passenger car with a small four-cylinder, fuel-efficient engine that could effectively compete with domestic and foreign models.

In January 1980, President Carter signed into law the Chrysler Corporation Loan Guarantee Act, which provided for up to $1.5 billion in loan guarantees, to be matched by U.S. and foreign banks, creditors, stockholders, suppliers, dealers, and others.[36] Under terms of the agreement, the government had warrants to buy 14.4 million shares of Chrysler stock at $13 per share. At that time Chrysler stock was selling for $7.50 per share, and later it declined to $4 per share. Chrysler was restored to financial health in 1982 when it showed a profit. Its stock price began to climb, reaching $30 per share in July 1983. The government sold the warrants back to Chrysler in September 1983 for $311 million.

The federal government has also aided entire industries. Even before the September 11, 2001, terrorist attacks, the U.S. airline industry faced significant financial difficulties due to its inherent instability. High levels of debt and high fixed costs for labor, fuel, and equipment mean that relatively small changes in the volume of air travel or in the cost of fuel have a major impact on profits. In 2000, the downturn in economic activity and increase in fuel prices contributed to shrinking airline profits and the bankruptcy of many small airlines (Tower Air, Pro Air Inc., Legend Airlines, National Airlines, Allegiant Air, Access Air, and others).[37] In 2001, before the terrorist strikes, United Airlines (the second largest in the United States) posted a loss of $605 million, and TWA and Midway Airlines failed.[38] Within an hour of the attacks, the Federal Aviation Administration ordered a ground stop for all air carrier (passengers and air cargo) and general aviation flights (September 11–13, 2001). Revenue passenger miles flown by large, certified air carriers declined from 67.5 billion in August 2001 to 38.2 billion in September.[39] The rebound was slow, with only 47.4 billion revenue passenger miles flown in December.

On September 22, 2001, President Bush signed into law the Air Transportation Safety and System Stabilization Act, which provided compensation to domestic air carriers for losses they incurred as a result of the mandatory grounding of aircraft in connection with the September 11, 2001, terrorists attacks and sought to maintain essential air carrier service. Title I of the act included $5 billion in compensation for direct losses incurred as a result of the federal ground stop and up to $10 billion in loan guarantees or other federal credit instruments to such air carriers. It established the Air Transportation Stabilization Board (ATSB) to issue the credit instruments.[40] To compensate the government for its risk in guaranteeing the loans, the ATSB collected fees, and to participate in equity gains, it received warrants. The ATSB rejected some loan requests, including those of Frontier Flying Service and Vanguard Airlines,[41] but the outright grants were based on airline size. As of April 2002, American Airlines had received $583 million, United Airlines $644 million, and Delta Airlines $529 million. The tiny Flying Eagle Aviation received a mere $273,000. A total of $3.9 billion was paid to 348 air carriers.[42]

Title II of the act authorized the secretary of transportation to reimburse air carriers for the increased cost of insurance since the terrorist attacks. It also limited the industry's liability for losses in connection with the attacks to an aggregate of $100 million. Title III delayed the payment of airline-related excise taxes from November 2001 until November 2002. Even with the government compensation, the airlines' estimated losses from the 9/11 terrorist attacks are in excess of $7 billion, over $4 billion more than the losses expected from the downturn in economic activity.[43] In the first quarter of 2002, most of the major airlines, including American, Delta, US Airways, and United, reduced their seating capacity and suffered losses of more than $2 billion. In the wake of the attacks, only Southwest increased its seating capacity and showed a small profit.

In June 2002, US Airways, one of the nation's largest airlines, applied for a $900 million federal loan guarantee. In July 2002, the loan guarantee was approved contingent upon the company gaining concessions from labor and creditors. That did not happen, so in August 2002, US Airways filed for Chapter 11 bankruptcy protection, which allows companies to reorganize, often while management remains in place.

CONCLUSIONS

Economic and financial crises are common phenomena that are frequently associated with real estate booms and busts that spread to other sectors of the economy. In response to crises, governments intervene with a variety of techniques designed to promote economic stability, aid distressed firms, and reduce the cost of resolution. The most commonly used intervention techniques include long-term investments, provision of short-term liquidity, nationalization, selling all or parts of financial institutions, payoffs, and forbearance. Those techniques address the symptoms but not the causes of crises, which include excessive leverage on the part of borrowers and lenders, credit risk, interest rate risk, and improper securitization. Instead of simply reacting to crises, governments should play a more proactive role in the amelioration of the conditions known to lead to financial disruption.

Government's first and most important task during a crisis is to restore economic stability and promote economic growth. Subsequently, government should deal with the causes of the crisis. Reticence to do so may be costly in the long run. Inefficient banks may remain in business, bailouts may weaken managerial incentives, and a loose monetary policy to prevent banking losses can cause inflation or currency depreciation, both of which can be extremely costly. Most important, bailouts create a moral hazard problem when firms believe that they may be bailed out if they are in financial distress.[44]

Finally, today's bailouts may have planted the seeds of the next crisis. In its desire to minimize the recession, the Federal Reserve has increased the money supply at an enormous rate, and the government has poured billions of dollars into the economy. The end result may be high levels of inflation, high interest rates, and a weakened dollar leading to another major boom and bust cycle. Government must address the causes of the current crisis and take appropriate actions to mitigate future crises.

NOTES

1   U.S. Department of Commerce, *Business Statistics 1961–1988* (Washington, DC, December 1989), 65; and U.S. Bureau of the Census, *Economic Indicators* (Washington, DC, September 2008), 30.

2   Carl-Johan Lindgren, Gillian Garcia, and Matthew I. Saal, *Banking Soundness and Macroeconomic Policy* (Washington, DC: International Monetary Fund, 1996).

3   Andrew Sheng, *Bank Restructuring: Lessons from the 1980s* (Washington, DC: World Bank, 1996).

4   FDIC, *History of the Eighties — Lessons for the Future, vol. 1, An Examination of Banking Crises of the 1980s and Early 1990s* (Washington, DC, 1997).

5   William L. Seidman, "Lessons of the Eighties: What Does the Evidence Show," in FDIC, *History of the Eighties,* 58.

6   Philip F. Bartholomew and Benton E. Gup, "A Survey of Bank Failures, Near Failures, and Significant Incidents in the Foreign G-10 Countries Since 1980" (paper presented at the annual meeting of the International Trade and Finance Association, Porto, Portugal, May 21, 1997); and Benton E. Gup, *Bank Failures in the Major Trading Countries of the World: Causes and Remedies* (Westport, CT: Quorum Books, 1998).

7   George M. von Furstenberg, "Default Risk on FHA Insured Home Mortgages as a Function of the Terms of Financing: A Quantitative Analysis," *Journal of Finance* 24, no. 3 (June 1969): 459–77; George M. von Furstenberg, "The Investment Qual-

ity of Home Mortgages," *Journal of Risk and Insurance* 37 (September 1970): 437–45; and Kerry D. Vandell, "Default Risk Under Alternative Mortgage Instruments," *Journal of Finance* 33, no. 5 (December 1978): 1279–96.

8 Harvey Rosenblum et al., "Fed Intervention: Managing Moral Hazard in Financial Crises," *Economic Letter: Insights from the Federal Reserve Bank of Dallas* 3, no. 10 (October 2008).

9 Definitions are from the OECD Glossary of Statistical Terms, http://stats.oecd.org/glossary/.

10 Anita Raghavan and Mitchell Pacelle, "A Hedge Fund Falters, and Big Banks Agree to Ante Up $3.5 Billion," *Wall Street Journal*, September 24, 1998, interactive edition.

11 Carrick Mollenkamp et al., "Behind AIG's Fall, Risk Models Failed to Pass Real-World Test," *Wall Street Journal*, November 3, 2008.

12 For a discussion of bank fraud and bank failures, see Benton E. Gup, *Targeting Fraud: Uncovering and Deterring Fraud in Financial Institutions* (New York: McGraw-Hill, 1995).

13 Joseph G. Haubrich provides an interesting discussion of the relationships between bank growth, diversification, and risk in "Bank Diversification, Laws and Fallacies of Large Numbers," Working Paper 9417 (Federal Reserve Bank of Cleveland, December 1994), https://www.clevelandfed.org/research/workpaper/1994/wp9417.pdf. In very general terms, banks grow by adding risky loans. Using the weak law of large numbers, Haubrich shows that diversified banks have a reduced expected failure rate. However, they are not necessarily less risky overall.

14 Office of the Comptroller of the Currency, *OCC's Quarterly Report on Bank Trading and Derivatives Activities: Second Quarter 2008* (Washington, DC, 2008).

15 Senate Committee on Banking, Housing, and Urban Affairs, *Hearing: The New Basel Capital Accord Proposal*, 108th Cong., 1st sess., June 18, 2003.

16 Tier 2 is limited to no more than 100% of Tier 1 capital.

17 Arturo Estrella, "A Prolegomenon to Future Capital Requirements," *Economic Policy Review* (Federal Reserve Bank of New York) 1, no. 2 (July 1995): 1–12.

18 FDIC, *History of the Eighties*, 1:57.

19 In 1997, regulators added an "S" to CAMEL to create CAMELS. "S" stands for sensitivity. For additional information about CAMEL(S), see Timothy J. Curry, Peter J. Elmer, and Gary S. Fissel, "Using Market Information to Help Identify Distressed Institutions: A Regulatory Perspective," *FDIC Banking Review* 15, no. 3 (September 2003).

20 FDIC, *History of the Eighties*, 1:80.

21 Lindgren, Garcia, and Saal, *Banking Soundness*, Table 3; and Gup, *Bank Failures*.

22 FDIC, *Quarterly Banking Profile: All Institutions Performance Third Quarter 2008* (Washington, DC, 2008), Table III-A.

23 For further discussion of capital levels, see Alan Berger, Robert DeYoung, and Mark Flannery, "Why Do Large Banking Organizations Hold So Much Capital?" (paper presented at the Federal Reserve Bank of Chicago, Bank Structure Conference, May 2007); and Mark Carlson and Gretchen Weinbach, "Profits and Balance Sheet Developments at U.S. Commercial Banks in 2006," *Federal Reserve Bulletin*, 2007 (July): A47–A48.

24 FDIC, *Supervisory Insights*, 2005 (Winter).

25 Richard A. Brealey, "Basel II: The Route Ahead or Cul-de-Sac?" *Journal of Applied Corporate Finance* 18, no. 4 (Fall 2006): 34–43.

26 FDIC, *History of the Eighties*, 1:42.

27 Tim Carrington, "U.S. Won't Let 11 Biggest Banks in Nation Fail," *Wall Street Journal*, September 20, 1984.

28 Ross M. Robertson, *The Comptroller and Bank Supervision: A Historical Appraisal* (Washington, DC: Office of the Comptroller of the Currency, 1995).

29 Board of Governors of the Federal Reserve System, Press Release, September 16, 2008.

30 Matthew Karnitschnig and Liam Pleven, "Government, AIG Near a Pact to Scrap Original Rescue Deal," *Wall Street Journal*, November 10, 2008.

31 Marine Cole, "AIG's Losses Show Swaps Next Domino," *Financial Week*, February 18, 2008.

32 David Enrich, Carrick Mollenkamp, and Matthias Rieker, "Bailout Talks Accelerate for Ailing Citigroup," *Wall Street Journal*, November 24, 2008.

33 For additional details, see Benton E. Gup, *Bank Failures*.

34 U.S. General Accounting Office, *Guidelines for Rescuing Large Failing Firms and Municipalities*, GAO/GGD-84-34 (Washington, DC, March 29, 1984).

35 U.S. Department of the Treasury, Emergency Loan Guarantee Board, *Second Annual Report* (Washington, DC, 1973), 6.

36 *Chrysler Corporation Loan Guarantee Act of 1979*, Public Law 96-185, 96th Cong., (January 7, 1980). For additional information about Chrysler, see: Ed Wallace, "Why Chrysler Failed," *BusinessWeek*, May 5, 2009, http://www.businessweek.com/lifestyle/content/may2009/bw2009055_922626.htm.

37 Standard and Poor's, "Airlines Industry Survey," March 29, 2001.

38 Laurence Zuckerman, "United Airlines Ousts Chief," *NYTimes.com*, October 29, 2001, http://www.nytimes.com/2001/10/29/business/29AIR.html.

39 U.S. Department of Transportation, Research and Innovative Technology Administration, "Historical Air Traffic Data Monthly: Year 2001."

40 For more details about the ATSB, see U.S. Department of the Treasury, "Air Transportation Stabilization Board," http://www.ustreas.gov/offices/domestic-finance/atsb/.

41 Frontier Flying Service Inc. should not be confused with Frontier Airlines Inc.

42 U.S. Department of Transportation, www.dot.gov/affairs/carrierpayments.htm.

43 Air Transport Association, *State of the U.S. Airline Industry: A Report on Recent Trends for U.S. Air Carriers, 2002* (Washington, DC: 2002); and John Schmeltzer, "United's Parent Company Posts $510 Million First-Quarter Loss," *Chicago Tribune*, April 20, 2002.

44 For additional details, see Asli Demirgüç-Kunt and Enrica Detragiache, "The Determinants of Banking Crises: Evidence from Developed and Developing Countries," IMF Working Paper No. 97/106 (Washington, DC: International Monetary Fund, July 1997).

CHAPTER THREE

The Evolution of the Reconstruction Finance Corporation as a Lender of Last Resort in the Great Depression

JOSEPH R. MASON

The Federal Reserve has come under attack in the last several decades for gradually adopting the more liberal philosophy of lending to distressed firms and industries. In the Great Depression, Federal Reserve assistance to weak financial intermediaries was almost nonexistent.[1] Many Federal Reserve officials held that "bank policy," that is, sterilized discount window lending and open bank assistance, provided untoward insulation from competitive market responses to economic adjustments.

Furthermore, the crises in the U.S. savings and loan and banking industries during the late 1980s and early 1990s reminded regulators that the insurance safety net underlying U.S. financial intermediaries is only effective in an environment of idiosyncratic bank failures. Once the public begins to mistrust the integrity of the industry as a whole, deposit insurance providers may experience a bout of illiquidity themselves, or at worst, bankruptcy. In the midst of the Thrift Crisis, this realization prompted a resurgence of interest into schemes to provide assistance to distressed financial intermediaries. Both the banking community and the Federal Deposit Insurance Corporation (FDIC) have therefore repeatedly considered the efficient scale and scope of open bank assistance.

The development of Federal Reserve and FDIC attitudes toward troubled financial intermediaries has accelerated the debate over the desirability of federally sponsored bank policy. At one end of the spectrum, Marvin Goodfriend and Robert King claim that bank policy is unnecessary, in that monetary policy can stabilize the macroeconomy while financial intermediaries are allowed to adjust to a new competitive environment. At the other extreme, Charles Goodhart proposes that all troubled banks should be granted assistance since "the distinction between illiquidity and insolvency is a myth."[2]

The lodestone of bank policy, hailed as the first large-scale successful application, is thought to be the Reconstruction Finance Corporation (RFC). But the RFC was a creature of its own economic and political environment, so recreating it in another environment would be problematic. Moreover, while the RFC was probably indispensible for addressing specific local banking crises and myriad stimulus programs, systematic testing in academic literature has called into doubt its purported success in keeping banks open. Hence, the present chapter puts the RFC into economic and political context, demonstrating the specific influences that shaped this behemoth.

The first section of this chapter reviews some of the history of the Federal Reserve System (the Fed) before 1930. The early Fed had no powers to resolve banks and so did not concern itself with individual bank difficulties. While bank failures were recognized as a growing problem in 1931, President Hoover had strong opinions about the shape of a bank assistance agency, leading his administration to experiment with a cooperative mechanism, as described in the second section of this chapter. The third section details the stiff bank assistance debate that arose between bankers and regulatory officials from different parts of the country. The regulatory debate fed into the legislative debate over the scope of the nascent RFC, which is described in the fourth section. Section five examines the rapid expansion of RFC powers and authority and the manner in which the RFC was used to both address local banking crises and fund New Deal programs. The sixth section describes the eventual demise of the RFC. The seventh section concludes.

THE INCIDENCE OF BANKING CRISES IN THE 1920S AND 1930S

Early banking crises of the 1920s were primarily regional affairs, so that even the large numbers of bank failures (referred to in some regulatory reporting as suspensions) did not give cause for regulatory concern. The Midwest, particularly Illinois, was especially impacted. Part of the reason for the impact was political. In 1923 the Illinois legislature passed an act to prohibit branch banking within the state. As the real estate boom and popularity of the automobile following World War I opened up new areas for residential development within Illinois, new independent banks were established. But the branch restriction meant that many of these new banks were poorly diversified with respect to loans and investments, often having lent significant proportions of their capital to local developers. Following the demise of many poorly diversified rural banks in the 1920s, both farm and commercial property markets underwent a period of severe deflation during the early 1930s, with the result that the weakened banking industry in Illinois was poised for a series of panics that would eventually undermine the confidence necessary for fractional reserve banking.[3]

Bank suspensions seemed to have reached a peak in 1926 and declined for several years thereafter. In 1929 the number of suspensions rose once again, and in 1930 the number was more than double that of the previous year, rising far above the peak of 1926. The first banking crisis of the Great Depression, in the last two months of 1930, resulted in the closure of over six hundred banks, with deposits of about $550 million,[4] and culminated with the closing of the Bank of United States in New York City, with over $200 million in deposits. It is important to realize that the failure of the Bank of United States was an anomaly during this period, as most of the failures were centered in the midwestern states of Missouri, Indiana, and Illinois, as well as Arkansas and North Carolina.[5]

Between April and August 1931, the occasional crises remained strictly regional in scope. There existed little or no domestic currency hoarding in six of the twelve Federal Reserve districts, and bank suspensions took place mainly in the Chicago and Minneapolis districts, where banks were forced to sell off large proportions of their secondary reserves in order to maintain liquidity. In the Chicago area, a crisis of confidence spread among outlying suburban banks suffering from declines in real estate values. More than one-third of all bank suspensions in the United States, nearly two hundred during the April–August 1931 crises, were in the Chicago District. Deposit losses for failed banks in the Chicago District during June 1931 amounted to 64% of the total losses for the entire country.[6]

Those regional crises ebbed with Britain's announcement of its departure from gold convertibility on September 21, 1931. While a nationwide crisis followed, bank runs were still targeted toward "particular banks that were known to be weak or among specialized banks such as savings banks and trust companies."[7] Furthermore, the adverse effects of the crisis still varied from region to region. Suspensions and deposits in closed banks remained high in Chicago, but "the New York market absorbed without dire consequences the demand for funds generated by the loss of depositor confidence in the interior of the country."[8] There existed no crisis in the New York District as measured by the number of suspensions or deposits in closed banks, although Elmus Wicker notes that "deposits in closed banks in New York were larger than in six [of the eleven] other Districts."[9]

Despite the persistently high level of suspensions and deposit losses in the Chicago District, there is no evidence that the Federal Reserve Bank of Chicago took positive action to keep any of the distressed banks open through direct intervention. Indeed, most losses in the Chicago District were attributed to overexposure of bank portfolios to real estate loans. Sue Patrick points out that:

> although the [Federal Reserve Act] permitted a Reserve Bank to examine a member, it could not expel any bank unless the Reserve had evidence the bank was violating the Federal Reserve Act. Nor did a Reserve Bank have the right to refuse to make a loan to a bank simply because the Reserve disliked the bank's management. This made it almost impossible for Reserve Banks to correct poor management.[10]

For this reason, "system officials did not recognize any strong obligation to maintain the solvency of the banking system."[11] During the crises of 1931, no assistance was offered other than to discount eligible paper of the member banks. No Federal Reserve accommodation whatsoever was available to non-member banks.

As bank failures escalated, the Federal Reserve remained generally uninterested. Milton Friedman and Anna Schwartz contend that:

> the [Federal Reserve] Board reported the melancholy figures of suspensions, properly classified as member and non-member, national and state banks, and confined itself to noting that suspensions were in disproportionate number of

non-member rather than member banks, of banks in small communities rather than in large, and of banks in agricultural rather than industrial areas.[12]

The effects of the number of suspensions on depositors or confidence in the banking system as a whole were not addressed. It was widely held that bank failures during this period were largely a result of "bad management and the economic conditions which have resulted from [World War I]."[13]

For many remaining banks, however, depositors' confidence had been breached, forcing bankers to take swift action to maintain liquidity. Gerald Epstein and Thomas Ferguson describe how banks, from October 1929 to March 1933, shifted their portfolios out of loans and into short-term assets, especially government securities, in order to maintain high levels of liquidity.[14] Unfortunately for these banks, excessive demand for short-term assets pushed yields down, eventually forcing them below zero in October and November 1932.[15] Some observers even claimed that declining yields squeezed margins of intermediation to the point that banks turned away new deposits since deposit rates were higher than yields on the banks' asset portfolios.[16] Despite high reserve ratios, continuous pressure on banks caused liquid assets in even the largest U.S. banks to decline to precariously low levels in 1932. Increasingly, the federal government was pressured to respond to requests by banks and the public to do something to mitigate the effects of the crisis.[17]

PRELUDE TO THE RECONSTRUCTION FINANCE CORPORATION: THE NATIONAL CREDIT CORPORATION

Since bank failures still seemed idiosyncratic, however, federal officials did not see a reason to extend direct government aid. In September 1931, therefore, Hoover met with Eugene Meyer, chairman of the Federal Reserve Board and former board member of the War Finance Corporation (WFC), to propose a private corporation that would provide emergency funds to stem liquidity crises: the National Credit Corporation (NCC).

Membership in the NCC was to be voluntary, and the funding would come from the bankers themselves, with the government providing only legal recognition of the organization. Hoover's proposal was met with restrained enthusiasm, however, as Meyer "did not share the president's faith in the financial community."[18] Meyer urged Hoover to revive the

WFC, which had been used during World War I to "augment capital investment markets and make loans to war industries," that is, banks, building and loan associations, and public utilities.[19]

Despite Meyer's insistence, Hoover preferred that the bankers work together to provide a solution. It is uncertain to what extent President Hoover actually disliked the idea of reestablishing the WFC, except that he preferred to limit direct government intervention to periods of war and did not desire to undertake the resurrection of the WFC until his proposed NCC had proven a failure. By putting off the establishment of a WFC-based organization, Hoover also avoided convening a special session of Congress to seek approval for the legislation, which he felt would only add panic to the ongoing banking crisis.[20]

At Hoover's insistence, Meyer persuaded a group of New York bankers to meet with the president to discuss the idea. The bankers, however, aware of Hoover's intentions, "privately agreed during the automobile trip from New York not to provide any emergency credit agency. They wanted the federal government to channel its resources directly into the nation's financial establishments" by reestablishing the WFC and providing assistance for railroad bond prices in order to strengthen banks' holdings.[21] Hoover finally convinced the bankers to establish the NCC on the provision that if it failed, an organization modeled on the WFC would be forthcoming.[22]

The NCC was formally organized on October 13, 1931, endorsed by the American Bankers Association and, later, the Investment Bankers Association. Participating banks were required to subscribe to an amount of NCC notes not less than 2% "of their respective net demand and time deposits as of the call last preceding October 14, 1931." The corporation was to consist of many regional subsidiaries, which would oversee lending in their respective districts. Banks would only be liable for losses incurred from the lending activities in their own districts.[23]

Although the NCC was loosely based on the clearinghouse structure of the pre-Federal Reserve era, certain features of the NCC nearly guaranteed its failure. First, the weakest banks, which were in the greatest need of assistance, often were unable to put up the required 2% for membership. Thus the NCC was unable to address the vast majority of bank failures. Second, the regional subsidiaries contained hundreds, or even thousands, of banks, whereas the pre–Fed-era clearinghouses typically oversaw only twenty or thirty. Bankers participating in the system could, therefore, not easily monitor the behavior of others and lacked an incentive to do so. This aspect led to the third weakness: adverse selection. Because there existed no clear way to monitor other banks in the NCC and no disciplinary devices (such as exclusion) were in place, weak banks could rationally expect to join the organization to receive subsidized loans that could then be used to invest in high-risk assets in a "bid for resurrection." Sound banks, unwilling to assume the risks of these weaker banks, were reluctant to lend under the provisions of the NCC.[24]

Soon after the organization's inception, President Hoover became dissatisfied with delays in NCC assistance. Hoover's promise to reincarnate the WFC had created incentives for bankers to stifle the NCC lending process to obtain the form of assistance they thought necessary. Despite the dearth of NCC loans, bank failures soon slowed, and stock and bond prices rallied. Bankers and politicians took these movements as signs of the program's success. The NCC seemed to have increased public confidence, and the officers of the NCC hoped that the "agency could be dissolved without making any loans."[25]

Unfortunately, the favorable economic climate did not last. By late November bank suspensions resumed their pace, and securities prices declined. Hoover finally conceded defeat and worked with Meyer and other Fed officials to draft legislation creating the RFC.

The officers of the NCC moved almost immediately to liquidate the few loans that had actually been disbursed, but several exigencies delayed their progress. As the legislation empowering the RFC moved through Congress, "many [legislators] openly criticized the [NCC] and expressed misgivings about assisting people unwilling to help themselves." To protect their interests, bankers associated with the NCC became much more willing to authorize bank assistance loans after early December 1931. As passage of the RFC legislation became more certain, NCC members who previously took out bank assistance loans hoped that they could replace NCC funding with cheaper RFC loans. The NCC therefore lent over $140 million in January and February of 1932, compared with only $10 million in October and November of 1931.[26]

NCC lending may have helped reduce the impact of several small banking crises in the South during January and February of 1932. However, the failure of the NCC to provide adequate assistance to stimulate a national recovery was imminent. The NCC did not have the authority to lend to railroads to halt the continuing price deterioration of bonds held by most banks. Furthermore, small country banks, which were frequently those most in need of funds, often were unable to contribute the 2% subscription required for NCC membership. Additionally, the NCC provided no assistance to life insurance companies, savings banks, building and loan associations, and a host of other financial institutions that held the same sorts of frozen assets as commercial banks.[27]

THE REGULATORY DEBATE OVER FEDERAL RESERVE ASSISTANCE IN THE EARLY 1930S

Lester Chandler describes Federal Reserve System officials during the early 1930s as holding "sharply conflicting views concerning the System's responsibilities, its proper objectives, its powers, and the effects of its policies on the economy."[28] This divisiveness was fostered by the general wording of the Federal Reserve Act, which "practically assured a maximum amount of conflict and controversy within the System."[29] The polar extremes in the philosophical debate were held by the Federal Reserve Banks of New York and Chicago, whose respective geographic domains were impacted quite differently by the early banking crises during 1929–31.

The Federal Reserve Bank of New York was by far the Federal Reserve System's leading advocate of the use of monetary policy to control the economy. However, the Federal Reserve Bank of New York's overzealous attempts to take a leadership role in such matters during a period of centralization of power at the Federal Reserve Board led to the alienation of the board and the banks. Governor McDougal of the Federal Reserve Bank of Chicago took the opposite view with respect to the desirability of the use of monetary policy for economic stabilization. McDougal first took issue with the Federal Reserve Bank of New York's strong desire to control monetary policy at the June 1916 Governors' Conference. By 1927, McDougal's unwillingness to conform to easy-money policy originating in the Federal Reserve Bank of New York to promote international central bank cooperation led to a direct mandate from the board to reduce the Federal Reserve Bank of Chicago's discount rate.[30]

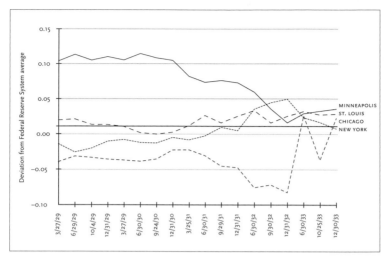

Figure 3.1   Ratio of investments to loans and investments, 1929–1933

McDougal felt that domestic and, more important, local economic conditions should take precedence over international considerations. In July 1930, the midwestern reserve banks firmly opposed the Federal Reserve Bank of New York's requests for an open market purchase program.[31] McDougal remained an adamant opponent of open market purchases throughout the crises of 1931, after which many of the other Federal Reserve banks throughout the country began to share the belief that further open market purchases would simply cause reserves to accumulate in reserve center banks. Other Federal Reserve banks soon realized that as regional crises progressed, reserve city banks were seeking liquidity by calling loans and investing in short-term government securities. Open market purchases, therefore, simply served to push the yields on such securities lower.

Figures 3.1 and 3.2 show that the shift in bank portfolios into government notes and bills began much earlier in the Chicago Federal Reserve District than elsewhere. The Federal Reserve Bank of New York's attempts to instigate a more active program of open market purchases waned in late 1932 as banks in that district began to accumulate large amounts of short-term government paper, while the hoarding of governments in the St. Louis District was less pronounced over this period.

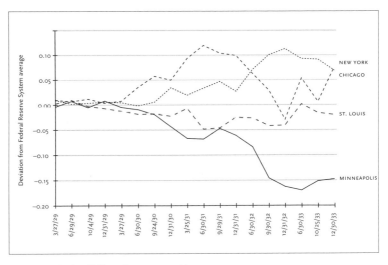

Figure 3.2   Ratio of bills and notes to total investments, 1929–1933

Figure 3.1 shows that banks in the Minneapolis District on aggregate held over 10% of their portfolios in investments until the end of 1930, when they began to divest heavily. Figure 3.2 suggests that the disinvestment of Minneapolis District banks was a result of an early panic, since levels of governments were drawn far below the Federal Reserve System average over 1931 and 1932. The massive flight to quality resulted in a precipitous decline in yields on notes and bills during this period, with negative yields resulting in late 1932.[32]

The policy of the Federal Reserve Bank of Chicago was that it was better to leave the eligible securities in the banks so that they could be used as collateral on loans, furthering credit expansion and preventing extreme declines in yields. McDougal was not against the provision of liquidity to bankers; rather he argued that "on general principles, he preferred to see the banks borrowing to secure funds." By early 1932, Governor Harrison of the Federal Reserve Bank of New York was forced to admit that banks' "attitudes had changed gradually since the last year in the face of the shrinkage in values" and that "banks were much more interested in avoiding possible losses than in augmenting their current income" through an expansion of the supply of credit.[33] This was as close as the Federal Reserve Bank of New York would come to disavowing their belief that monetary policy was an adequate stabilization tool for all economic crises.

THE LEGISLATIVE DEBATE AND THE RESULTING SCOPE OF THE RFC

Adolph J. Sabath, representative from the state of Illinois, first introduced a bill providing for relief for the banking industry early in 1930. Despite the successive waves of bank failures in the Midwest throughout the year, the bill did not gather popular support. Bank failures in the Midwest accelerated during 1930 primarily as a result of diminished solvency and reduced depositor confidence. Overexposure to illiquid farm mortgages and the lack of sufficient arrangements to repay depositors of insolvent institutions helped to ensure that the probability of runs remained high. Thus, by 1931, Sabath's bill contained provisions for

1. the creation of a Finance Corporation for assisting all industry, financial and otherwise;
2. the establishment of home loan banks or mortgage banks; and
3. broadening Federal Reserve rediscount eligibility.

These features would all eventually be embodied in the RFC or related legislation.[34]

By November 1931, it became apparent that the National Credit Corporation was a failure, and Hoover made plans to introduce new banking assistance legislation.[35] During congressional hearings on the creation of the RFC, geographic regions primarily determined boundaries of ideology for the debate. As was typical, the debate focused on differences in ideologies of New York and Chicago bankers. The main point of concern for the Chicago bankers was the eligibility of both various forms of collateral and different classes of banks for RFC loans, while the New York banks were primarily concerned with limiting their exposure to losses in the rest of the system.

Melvin Traylor, president of the First National Bank of Chicago, Illinois, personified the effects of the massive number of failures in that city during 1930–31. With firsthand experience, Traylor took issue with the mechanics of the bank failure process and its relation to the contemporary loss of confidence in the banking industry. Traylor's peremptory concern was to promote the formation of an organization to lend to closed and illiquid banks. Since June 1930, 51% of deposits in failed Chicago banks had been paid out, but only at the expense of banks emptying their note cases and borrowing against every available collateral. Succinctly stated, Traylor maintained that "if you are going to restrict your operation to collateral that is reasonably liquid and going to be paid in a reasonable time, then you are not going to reach the situation that needs help."[36]

Wilson Mills, chairman of the board of the Peoples Wayne County Bank of Detroit, Michigan, echoed Traylor's remarks, providing particularly acute insights to the concerns of the receivers of closed banks. To Mills, the provision of greater liquidity to the banking system was the key to regaining public confidence. According to Mills, a great many banks in the Chicago District had mortgages that were probably their best assets. Even if a mortgage is good, however, "it does not do the bank any good to have it when it closes its doors and goes into the hands of a receiver" since it is illiquid. When a bank closes and a receiver steps in,

> he finds that their best assets are already hypothecated to some other bank. A closed bank has had to do that in order to get funds to carry on, to pay its depositors. The receiver is faced right away with the question of . . . shall I liquidate that loan by sale of the [collateral] securities or shall I sit around and hope that the prices will go up? . . . Mean time the depositors do not get a nickel out of it.[37]

The attitude in New York, however, was a great deal more conservative. J. C. Trephagen, representative of the Bank of New York, maintained that lending to closed and illiquid banks "might be a mistake" and that "if the purposes of this bill are accomplished, and the operations of this corporation make themselves felt, the local banks will gladly lend to the failed banks." Trephagen continued:

> There are many securities today . . . which are normally salable, but which today cannot be sold. The banks know that, and as a consequence they hesitate to make further loans and get themselves in any less liquid position . . . A little money placed in the right kind of way in the right kind of loans would start the flow of credit through the banks again, and I think that is the essential thing.[38]

Trephagen's position was reiterated by Harry Ward, president of the Irving Trust Company, New York. Ward was primarily concerned with a "shrinkage in the supply of credit" resulting from the need for strong banks to attain high levels of liquidity in order to maintain credibility with correspondents.[39]

New York banks did not argue against the establishment of the RFC. Rather, they felt that the effective scale and scope of the institution needn't be as large as that favored by bankers from Illinois and other midwestern states. The resulting bill was somewhat of a compromise. Congress did not even consider the radical idea of recapitalizing banks proffered by some midwestern bankers, and they placed limits on the amount of loans that could be used to pay off deposits of closed banks. Beyond this, however, the bill only stipulated that loans be priced so as not to crowd out private investment and be "adequately secured." The resulting institution was thus given powers broad enough to meet the demands of midwestern bankers.[40]

THE INSTITUTIONAL HISTORY OF THE RECONSTRUCTION FINANCE CORPORATION

The banking industry's experience with the NCC led to "a growing appreciation of the fact that an [assistance] organization was needed not merely to provide liquidity for banks and railroads, but rather to assume the risk of loss—and the losses—in a situation wherein no one could give an assurance as to the date when adjustment would be completed."[41] In February 1932, the first Glass-Steagall Act, which liberalized Federal Reserve borrowing requirements and collateral types that could be held against Federal Reserve notes, passed through Congress.

Hoover's RFC opened for business that same month, on February 2, 1932, ready to lend directly to banks and railroads in order to forestall a widespread liquidity crisis. The RFC initially attempted to reduce the number of bank failures by infusing the system with liquidity through a policy of making loans to those "which cannot otherwise secure credit." Although the agency had full discretion to stipulate loan prices and length of maturity, there was a concern that RFC credit might tend to crowd out private investment. Thus RFC loans carried high interest rates (6%) and short maturities (six months) and took banks' best liquid assets as collateral. These loan policies were relaxed throughout the first year of the RFC.[42]

The RFC initially sold capital stock of $500 million, all subscribed by the United States of America and held by the secretary of the treasury.[43] The corporation was authorized to issue "notes, debentures, bonds, or other such obligations in an amount not exceeding three times its subscribed capital."[44] These additional obligations could be sold to the public or the Treasury of the United States. The amount of subscribed capital was increased several times over the 1930s as the responsibilities of the RFC mushroomed. The idea was for the RFC to be a true corporation, only vaguely controlled by Congress, despite the Treasury's capitalization.[45]

The board of directors was constructed to represent a diverse set of interests. The board initially included the secretary of the treasury, the governor of the Federal Reserve Board, and the farm loan commissioner as ex officio members and four directors appointed by the president and confirmed by the Senate. Directors appointed by the president had terms of five years.[46] The initial appointees to the board of directors of the RFC were Eugene Meyer, chairman of the Federal Reserve Board; Ogden Mills, secretary of the treasury; H. Paul Bestor, president of the Federal Farm Loan Bank; Charles G. Dawes, statesman; Harvey Couch, a banking and railroad executive; Jesse Jones, a banking and real estate executive; and Wilson McCarthy, a financial and agricultural executive.

Although the RFC's charter was granted for a ten-year period, lending activities were restricted to a period of one year, which could be extended by executive order. (Such an order was issued by Hoover on December 8, 1932, extending lending authority until January 21, 1934.) The temporary nature of the organization undoubtedly hindered its ability to restore public confidence since substantial uncertainty regarding the end of the crisis still existed.

The RFC was initially empowered to make loans to a variety of financial institutions as well as railroads, a decision that addressed the two main concerns of the erstwhile opponents of the NCC. But initial RFC lending policies were conservative to a fault. The high interest rates and strict collateral demands most likely increased the risk of default on remaining bank debt and undermined any stabilizing effect of assistance.[47] Although the RFC had legislative authority to extend maturities to three years, it was reluctant to do so and thereby relinquish greater control over borrowers. Despite such conservatism, the RFC authorized

NUMBER OF LOANS AUTHORIZED TO THE BANK	NUMBER OF BANKS	TOTAL AMOUNT OF BANK BORROWING FROM THE RFC	AVERAGE BANK LOAN AMOUNT FROM THE RFC
1	4,481	$ 358,077,401.04	$ 79,910.15
2	1,342	325,464,728.02	242,522.15
3	434	125,427,277.95	289,002.94
4	175	97,681,758.24	558,181.48
5	66	31,357,926.04	475,120.09
6	38	42,665,017.79	1,122,763.63
7	18	104,056,172.63	5,780,898.48
8	4	3,517,862.39	879,465.60
9	3	1,448,437.68	482,812.56
10	2	1,065,099.32	532,549.66
>10	4	6,806,275.50	126,042.14
TOTAL	6,567	$ 1,097,567,956.60	$ 167,133.84

Source: RFC monthly reports to Congress, various issues, and author's calculations.

Note: Includes only loans to open banks. Does not include loans to receivers or those made on preferred stock.

Table 3.1   Borrowing behavior of banks, February 1932–March 1933

$238 million in loans during the first two months of operation, $160 million of which went to banks and trust companies.[48]

Bank failures fell from 342 in January and 119 in February to 45 in March. However, the declining number of bank failures during this period may provide a somewhat misleading measure of the effectiveness of the RFC. Problem banks received forbearance, but not necessarily salvation. Of the more than $1 billion lent to banks prior to March 1933, nearly 70% went to banks borrowing more than once, and 15% to banks borrowing more than five times (see table 3.1). The most conspicuous episodes of repeat borrowing took place in Nevada and Michigan, two states that were hit especially hard during the banking crises that took place later in 1932 and at the beginning of 1933, perhaps indicating that the RFC simply forestalled the inevitable.[49]

FIRST EXPANSION OF RFC AUTHORITIES:
THE EMERGENCY RELIEF AND CONSTRUCTION ACT

Although the RFC was initially viewed as successful, its operations were soon embroiled in controversy over lending to "big business." In March 1932 the RFC lent over $23 million to the Missouri Pacific Railroad.

Then in June, the Central Republic Bank and Trust Company in Chicago, formerly owned by RFC chairman Charles Dawes, was granted a loan of $90 million to avert widespread bank failures throughout the Chicago area.[50] Largely because of these loans, the Emergency Relief and Construction Act (ERCA), effective July 21, 1932, provided that the RFC make monthly reports to Congress, including the names of borrowers and amounts lent, and refrain from lending to businesses recently associated with its directors.

Sue Patrick remarks that Hoover was never completely satisfied with the publicity of RFC loan recipients and did not sign the legislation until he "assured everyone that no publicity would occur while Congress was not in session."[51] But the Speaker of the House misinterpreted the legislation and during the summer congressional recess released the reports to the public and submitted them to the *New York Times* and other periodicals, raising the question of whether such publication would precipitate runs on borrowing banks.[52] (By 1933, the reports were only released as intended, while Congress was in session.)[53]

By July 1932 Hoover also faced considerable criticism regarding the effectiveness of RFC lending. Bankers, unhappy with strict RFC collateral and maturity requirements, failed to transform additional liquidity into lending opportunities for the general public. Banks preferred instead to continue increasing reserves and invest in liquid government securities. Since many of the complaints revolved around the conservatism of RFC lending policies, interest rates on RFC loans were dropped to 5.5%, and collateral requirements were relaxed.[54]

Throughout the first six months of RFC activity, Hoover and Eugene Meyer, chairman of the Federal Reserve Board, clashed constantly. Although Meyer testified during the hearings on the creation of an RFC that he felt the main purpose of such an organization was to foster confidence in the banking industry, he often stifled Hoover's attempts at "liberalization and creativity." During May, Meyer opposed Hoover's proposals to lend to states for unemployment relief. Later, Meyer forced the resignation of Henry Allen, Hoover's appointed press secretary for the RFC. Meyer's dictatorial attitude toward the RFC board introduced many power struggles among its members, and he soon tired of the bankers he was supposed to be assisting.[55] Thus in July 1932, ERCA provisions also called for the removal of two of the three ex-officio board members —

the governor of the Federal Reserve Board and the farm loan commissioner — and their replacement with appointed members, supposedly generating a more balanced consensus and unified purpose among the board of directors.[56]

Bills and proposals for welfare and relief programs of all kinds were presented to Congress during early 1932. Although Hoover remained true to his faith in generally market-based solutions, he began to ponder the limitations of his previous policies. The compromise he desired was soon proposed by a group of liberal Democrats. Federal relief would be provided through a program of loans for self-liquidating public works projects. Such projects would begin generating revenue for repayment of the loans immediately upon completion.[57] Thus the relief program would provide new jobs without resorting to outright grants. The idea for self-liquidating public works projects was amalgamated with some of the better ideas from earlier proposals and included in the ERCA.[58]

The ERCA increased the capital of the RFC by $1.8 billion and provided new outlets for lending powers already in existence. It also created three new divisions in the RFC: the Self-Liquidating Division, the Emergency Relief Division, and the Agricultural Credit Division. These divisions were empowered with certain capabilities:

1. $300 million in loans could be disbursed to states, territories, and municipalities for work relief and unemployment programs.
2. $1.5 billion in loans could be applied to self-liquidating projects undertaken by any type of organization ranging from states to private corporations. Most major infrastructure projects could qualify for these loans, provided that they could be made "self-supporting and financially solvent."
3. Loans could be made to finance sales of agricultural surpluses to foreign markets (the RFC could only be used as a lender of last resort in this respect).
4. Loans could be made to promote the "orderly marketing of agricultural commodities and livestock produced in the United States."
5. Regional agricultural credit corporations could be created in the twelve Federal land-bank districts. These regional corporations could make loans for crop and livestock production and also rediscount with the RFC or Federal Intermediate Credit Banks.[59]

On July 22, 1932, the RFC was required by a further amendment to allocate to the secretary of the treasury $125 million to purchase the stock of twelve newly created Federal Home Loan Banks charged with rediscounting home mortgages held by building and loan associations.[60]

During the months prior to the November 1932 election, the Hoover administration felt confident that the banking community was finally beginning to respond to the stimulus programs promoted by the RFC. Member bank borrowings were at their lowest point in a year, and reserves were at their highest level since July 1931. Deposits in Federal Reserve member banks also rose, from $24.7 million in July to $25.3 million in October. The number of bank failures dropped steadily from 151 in June to 67 in September. Securities prices in general, as well as railroad and utility prices, seemed to be on a healthy rebound. Applications for RFC loans had diminished significantly by October, and during that month repayments of previous loans exceeded disbursements for the first time ever.[61]

Despite the improvements noted above, banks still seemed reluctant to undertake commercial lending. Banks preferred to invest in government securities, and commercial loans were still below their 1928 levels. The RFC undertook a program of moral suasion to convince bankers to relinquish their fears of illiquidity and resume lending. However, the program ended abruptly as the RFC realized that the Chicago panic of June 1932 did not signal the nadir of the crisis, but only the inception.[62]

The revolutionary expansion of the powers of the government through the ERCA did not immediately promote economic recovery or even distract public criticism during the months prior to the election. Within two weeks of the passage of ERCA, states had applied for over two-thirds of the available funds. RFC officials slowed applications in order to conserve some of the authorized funds, attracting derision from state politicians. Furthermore, many of the projects authorized under the self-liquidating division involved long planning horizons so that construction could not even begin until after the election. Because of these and other circumstances the ERCA earned Hoover little political capital. Hoover won a mere fifty-nine electoral votes during the November 1932 presidential election, thirty-six of these coming from Pennsylvania, a state whose governor voiced the loudest criticisms of the RFC in the preceding months.[63]

The extended powers of the RFC also did not stop the acceleration of regional bank panics during the period between the election and inauguration.[64] The economic rebound that manifested itself over the course of several months fell apart on the eve of the election. Banks that had received RFC assistance began to fail en masse, and several states declared banking holidays, buying time to sort out their troubles. This movement was at least exacerbated, if not in a sense caused by, Roosevelt's refusal to commit to a position on currency devaluation. A run on the dollar ensued, leading bankers and government officials to urge Hoover to declare a bank holiday before the inauguration. Hoover, unsure of the legality of such a maneuver, balked at issuing such a proclamation.[65]

In addition to the uncertainty surrounding bank illiquidity and currency devaluation, depositors were also concerned about bank fraud during this period. On February 21, 1933, the chairman of the board of National City Bank, Charles Mitchell, had been called as a key witness at the Pecora hearings in Washington. Mitchell revealed questionable practices at one of the nation's most respected banks. By March 3, 1933, more than 5,500 banks, with combined deposits of over $3 billion, had suspended operations, and only a handful of states were left without some sort of restriction on banking. By March 5, all forty-eight states and the District of Columbia had imposed various types of moratoria on banking within their borders (table 3.2).[66] Thus few were surprised when Roosevelt imposed a nationwide three-day moratorium on banking on March 6, 1933.

THE EMERGENCY BANKING ACT AND THE GLASS-STEAGALL ACT OF 1933 RESTORE THE BANKING SYSTEM

Soon after the bank holiday moratorium took effect, policymakers in Washington drafted legislation to restructure the banking system and its constituent components. The Emergency Banking Act (officially titled the Emergency Banking Relief Act) was finalized at 3:00 a.m. on March 9, 1933, and signed into law by President Roosevelt by 8:36 that evening.[67]

The majority of the Emergency Banking Act consisted of legislation left over from the Hoover administration. The act consisted of five sections, three of which are of particular importance. Title I formally

STATE	ACTION	DATE EFFECTIVE
Alabama	Closed until further notice.	3/1
Arizona	Closed until March 12.	3/2
Arkansas	Closed until March 7.	3/2
California	Almost all closed until March 9.	3/1
Colorado	Closed until March 8.	3/4
Connecticut	Closed until March 7.	3/4
Deleware	Closed indefinitely.	3/4
District of Columbia	Three banks limited to 5 percent [withdrawals], nine banks invoke sixty days notice.	2/28
Florida	Withdrawals restricted to 5 percent plus $10 until March 8.	3/4
Georgia	Mostly closed until March 7, closing optional.	3/3
Idaho	Some closed until March 18, closing optional.	3/2
Illinois	Closed until March 8, then to be opened on 5 percent restriction basis for 5 days.	3/4
Indiana	About half restricted to 5 percent indefinitely.	2/26
Iowa	Closed "temporarily."	3/4
Kansas	Restricted to 5 percent withdrawals indefinitely.	
Kentucky	Mostly restricted to 5 percent withdrawals until March 11.	3/1
Louisiana	Closing mandatory until March 7.	3/1
Maine	Closed until March 7.	3/4
Maryland	Closed until March 6.	2/25
Massachusetts	Closed until March 7.	2/14
Michigan	Mostly closed, others restricted to 5 percent indefinitely; Upper Peninsula banks open.	
Minnesota	Closed "temporarily."	3/1
Mississippi	Restricted to 5 percent indefinitely.	3/1
Missouri	Closed until March 7.	3/4
Montana	Closed until further notice.	3/4
Nebraska	Closed until March 8.	3/2
Nevada	Closed until March 8, also schools.	
New Hampshire	Closed subject to further proclamation.	3/4
New Jersey	Closed until March 7.	3/3
New Mexico	Closed until March 8.	3/3
New York	Closed until March 7.	3/4
North Carolina	Some banks restricted to 5 percent withdrawals.	
North Dakota	Closed temporarily.	3/4
Ohio	Mostly restricted to 5 percent withdrawals indefinitely.	2/27
Oklahoma	All closed until March 8.	3/2
Oregon	All closed until March 7.	3/2
Pennsylvania	Mostly closed until March 7, Pittsburgh banks open.	3/4
Rhode Island	Closed March 4.	3/4
South Carolina	Some closed, some restricted, all on own initiative.	
South Dakota	Closed indefinitely.	
Tennessee	A few closed, others restricted, until March 9.	3/1
Texas	Mostly closed, others restricted to withdrawals of $15 daily until March 8.	3/2
Utah	Mostly closed until March 8.	
Vermont	Closed until March 7.	3/4
Virginia	All closed until March 8.	3/2
Washington	Some closed until March 7.	3/2
West Virginia	Restricted to 5 percent monthly withdrawals indefinitely.	3/3
Wisconsin	Closed until March 17.	3/3
Wyoming	Withdrawals restricted to 5 percent indefinitely.	3/3

Table 3.2   Status of state bank holidays as of March 5, 1933

[Source: Quoted in *Commercial and Financial Chronicle*, March 11, 1933, pp. 1481–7, 1670–4.]

legitimized Roosevelt's power under the Trading with the Enemy Act of 1917 to declare a national banking holiday. Title II, also known as the Bank Conservation Act, provided that conservators be appointed to national banks deemed unsound, as judged by federal examiners.[68] Title III granted the RFC permission to purchase a special class of preferred stock with full voting rights in any "national banking association or any State bank or trust company in need of funds for capital purposes in connection with the organization or reorganization of such association."[69]

The preferred stock purchased by the RFC was subject to some rather strict provisions. First, the preferred stock paid senior dividends of 6% per annum and was senior to all other stock upon liquidation of the firm. All other stock dividends were limited to a specified maximum, and remaining earnings were devoted to a preferred stock retirement fund. In addition, the stock was not subject to double-liability requirements. The stock could be resold to the public at the discretion of the RFC and carried voting rights that were often used to direct the institution toward solvency and profitability.[70]

The RFC was prohibited from purchasing more than 49% of the total outstanding voting stock in any one bank. However, it often owned the largest voting block in the company. Thus the RFC had effective control of many of the institutions in which it had investments. In several situations, the RFC used this control to replace officers and significantly alter the business practices of the institution. The earliest and most prominent intervention was that involving Continental Illinois National Bank and Trust Company of Chicago. However, other prominent banks were assured that the situation at Continental Illinois was due to a combination of unusual circumstances and would not be repeated without due cause.[71]

Using the newly conferred powers contained in the Emergency Banking Act, Roosevelt announced a scheme by which banks were allowed to reopen according to licenses issued by the secretary of the treasury. An executive order dated March 10, 1933, commanded the secretary of the treasury to "license any member of the Federal Reserve System which could obtain endorsement of its soundness from its district Reserve bank; state banking authorities could reopen non-member banks at their discretion."[72]

Roosevelt presented his plan to the nation during his first "fireside chat" on March 12. Federal Reserve member banks possessing licenses from the Treasury were allowed to reopen on March 13 if they were located within reserve cities. If openings proceeded in an orderly fashion on the thirteenth, licensed member banks located in cities with active clearinghouse associations could open on March 14. Again, assuming all went well on the fourteenth, the remaining licensed banks were allowed to open on March 15. At the end of the day on March 15, nearly 70% of the 18,390 banks in operation on March 3 had reopened, including 5,038 of the existing 6,816 Federal Reserve member banks.[73]

The RFC underwent a major transformation during the Roosevelt era. Two of the board members, Atlee Pomerene and Charles Miller, were appointed by Hoover during the congressional recess of August 1932 and had not yet been confirmed by Congress. Apparently, neither of these men cared for Roosevelt, so they retired. Gardner Cowles also resigned during the first month of the Roosevelt administration, ostensibly for political reasons, and secretary of the treasury Ogden Mills was replaced as ex officio member by the new secretary, William Woodin. The vacancies had to be filled by Republicans; so when Jesse Jones, a respected Texas banker and former board member who was now appointed chair, only came up with one recommendation, Roosevelt filled the other two with personal appointments.[74]

The new board was not only imbued with the power of equity investment but also had a much more dynamic sense of activism than before. It immediately relaxed loan collateral requirements further and cut loan interest rates by 1%. Furthermore, the RFC joined the Treasury and the comptroller in actively reorganizing what was left of the banking system. A newfound sense of purpose permeated the RFC, and the dynamic board of directors channeled all available resources toward reopening banks. Banks that did not reopen immediately were often placed in the hands of conservators according to Title II of the Emergency Banking Act.[75] A total of 4,215 banks were placed in the hands of conservators. Of these, 1,108 were national banks, 148 state member banks, and the rest non-member banks.[76] These banks constituted two basic groups: those that were judged to have "impaired assets but could reopen with large-scale RFC [assistance]" and those that clearly would have to be liquidated. Over 1,100 of these banks were liquidated outright during 1933, leaving the other 3,100 to be reorganized with RFC assistance. Conservators made ample use of RFC loan programs as well as the new powers to purchase preferred stock conferred under Title III of the Emergency Banking Act.[77]

The RFC and the comptroller relied on three methods to restore unopened banks: capital correction, creditor waiver, and "Spokane sale."

The capital correction method was used in the simplest cases, where banks simply needed an increased capital buffer. Often such cases were resolved with the provision of long-term capital through RFC preferred stock purchases.[78] Sometimes, as with Continental Illinois, the RFC imposed their voting rights to reorganize the bank's management as well, although such actions were rare.

Banks restructured through creditor waivers were typically insolvent, possessing appraised assets in amounts less than their liabilities. In order to maintain bank operations in the short term, the RFC typically lent funds to give banks time to "eliminate that portion of liabilities which exceeded assets." Usually such adjustment was made by "persuading banks' creditors to sign waivers of a percentage of their deposits or other claims," which also acted as a show of good faith from debt holders to the RFC. Once the balance of assets and liabilities was reestablished, preferred stock was then purchased in these banks to provide a better capital foundation for the firm.[79]

A Spokane sale was a more drastic solution for problem banks. A cross between a reorganization and a liquidation, Spokane sales were used for banks that were judged vital to the community but were deeply insolvent. In such cases, assessments on shareholders could not provide enough cash to pay off creditors. Therefore, bank assets were sold in bulk to an existing bank or a company established exclusively for their liquidation, after which the proceeds would be used to pay at least a proportion of creditors' demands. "After the sale and distribution, a receiver could liquidate the old bank and collect stock assessments." Thus the bank was liquidated in a Spokane sale, but depositors received their funds in a more timely manner than otherwise, and the bank, or portions of it, could be purchased by another institution. The Spokane sale was the only one of the three forms of reorganization that was used before the bank holiday. Previously the most liberal form of restructuring, the Spokane sale was now the most harsh.[80]

The RFC clearly took an active role in the rehabilitation of unsound banks. However, in the months following the holiday, banks that were not in the hands of conservators were reluctant to take full advantage of the newly liberalized RFC assistance programs. Barrie Wigmore points out that although some banks did not feel financial pressures during this period, such examples were rare. Even the largest banks in the country faced intense pressure on earnings and stock prices. Chase's stock hit a low of 13% of its highest 1929 price, and National City, 8%. However, during the first three weeks of the preferred stock program, the RFC made investments in only four banks, most as part of larger restructuring plans. During the second quarter of 1933, the RFC authorized preferred stock purchases in only fifty banks nationwide.[81]

Although the Banking Act of 1933, commonly known as the Glass-Steagall Act of 1933, did not alter the RFC's operating procedures, it provided a focal point for RFC bank assistance programs that was much more specific than the earlier goal of assisting banks suffering liquidity crises. Passed on June 16, this second Glass-Steagall Act provided various reforms with respect to branch banking, securities affiliates, and deposit insurance. Most significantly for the RFC, the act strove to strengthen confidence in the banking industry through the provision of deposit insurance on a national level.

Early deposit insurance schemes had proved inadequate as a direct result of their inability to diversify beyond some tightly constrained geographic area. The new Federal Deposit Insurance Corporation (FDIC) intended to combat this shortcoming through a truly nationwide system of deposit insurance. In so doing, however, the plan relied strongly upon the membership of all the nation's banks. All Federal Reserve member banks were required to subscribe to the FDIC, and non-member banks were allowed to join if they could prove solvency before the date the program took effect, January 1, 1934.[82]

During his fireside chats, Roosevelt promised the public that only solvent banks would reopen after the holiday. However, in examiners' haste to open as many banks as possible, they sometimes overestimated the value of bank assets. Thus by June 1933, the RFC was not only busy trying to reopen banks but also assisting those shaky banks that slipped past examiners. Jesse Jones estimated that over five thousand banks that reopened after the holiday "required considerable added capital to make them sound."[83] The RFC and the Federal Reserve realized that the unsound nature of these banks precluded FDIC membership on January 1, 1934, but Roosevelt wanted them to join on that date to ensure public confidence in the system.[84]

The RFC could exert considerable influence over banks that had not reopened since the holiday. These banks often took on assistance packages of preferred stock investments and loans rather readily as these measures were necessary if the bank was to continue operations. The unsound banks that had already reopened, however, presented Roosevelt and the RFC with a significant problem. Open banks were reluctant to participate in the preferred stock program because they thought RFC assistance signaled their unsound condition to the public. The RFC had little power to force these banks to participate.

In September, Jesse Jones, chairman of the RFC, addressed the American Bankers Association in Chicago. Jones rebuked bankers for their reluctance to participate in the preferred stock program while fully realizing the implications of their banks' inadequate capital positions and strongly urged all the leading banks in the United States to sell preferred stock to the RFC "so that depositors would not be induced to switch out of ... banks when [recipients'] names were published." The appeal to the American Bankers Association convention seemed to have had some impact on the bankers, and the number of applications received daily at the RFC increased substantially. In time, nearly all the banks sold stock to the RFC, although several sold only small amounts and immediately repaid them.[85]

In response to a backlog of assistance applications, on October 23, 1933, the RFC created the Non-Member Preferred Stock Board to handle the most delicate cases: more than 2,500 non–Federal Reserve member banks whose financial positions were still unsubstantiated by the Federal Reserve or the secretary of the treasury. At the same time, dividend and interest rates were lowered to 4%, inspiring even more banks to participate in RFC programs.[86] By November 1933, RFC applications were being sorted in a manner of triage. Banks "whose assets appeared to equal 90 percent of their total deposits and other liabilities exclusive of capital" were urged to seek private buyers for their stock in the belief that otherwise the RFC could end up owning a sizable portion of the banking industry. Banks that could not meet these requirements were put in what Jones refers to as the "hospital," awaiting the arrangement of more complex assistance packages.[87]

By December 15, 1933, there existed more than two thousand open banks in the hospital. With only two weeks until the deadline for FDIC membership, the RFC began to seek quick solutions. After a fruitless appeal to the Senate Committee on Banking and Currency, the RFC sought to soften the deadline. On December 28, Jones met with Secretary of the Treasury Morgenthau[88] to propose a compromise: if Morgenthau would certify the hospitalized banks as solvent, Jones guaranteed they would be so within six months. The hospitalized banks were thus recapitalized in a more orderly fashion than otherwise would have occurred, and another possible crisis of confidence was avoided.[89] "On January 1 Walter Cummings announced that the FDIC had accepted 13,423 banks as members and had rejected only 141."[90]

By March 1934 the RFC had purchased preferred stock in nearly half the commercial banks in the United States.[91] By June 1935, these RFC investments made up "more than one third of all outstanding capital in the entire [U.S.] banking system."[92] Figures 3.3 and 3.4 show that, at the peak, the RFC had outstanding loans of some $1.5 billion (about $25 billion in today's dollars). After recapitalizing the hospitalized institutions, RFC bank programs predominantly focused their attention on liquidating their stakes in the industry in an orderly fashion. During this period the RFC largely shifted its attention from assisting the banking industry in particular to facilitating a general recovery by providing loans and preferred stock investments to all industries. Upon the RFC's liquidation in 1953, these functions were taken up by the Small Business Administration (SBA), an agency specifically created to carry on the legacy of the RFC in this respect.

THE RFC IN THE AFTERMATH OF THE GREAT DEPRESSION

In 1934 Secretary of the Treasury Morgenthau successfully pressured the RFC to cut back assistance in order to help balance the budget. However, by midyear Morgenthau had to rescind his request because of pressures from the railroad industry. By the beginning of 1935 an economic expansion was under way, and President Roosevelt and Morgenthau "were adamant about reducing the budget deficit" and liquidating the RFC.[93]

Due to Morgenthau's persistence, the RFC stopped accepting applications for preferred stock and capital note purchases on July 15, 1935. "On November 12, 1935, in a speech to the American Bankers' Association, Jones announced that the bank emergency was over."[94] Banks that sold preferred stock to the RFC to help reduce adverse effects of publicity were the first to repurchase their equity. By the end of 1935,

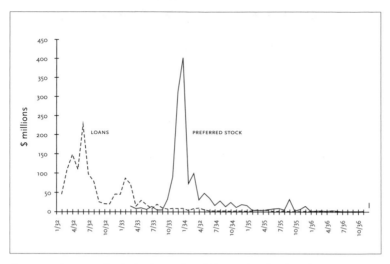

Figure 3.3   Amounts of authorizations under RFC loan and preferred stock programs, monthly, 1932–1936   [Source: RFC monthly reports to Congress, various issues.] [Note: Figures include only loans to open banks. Does not include loans to receivers or those made on preferred stock. The RFC preferred stock program began in March 1933. Preferred stock includes investments made through notes and debentures to banks in states that prohibited preferred stock investments.]

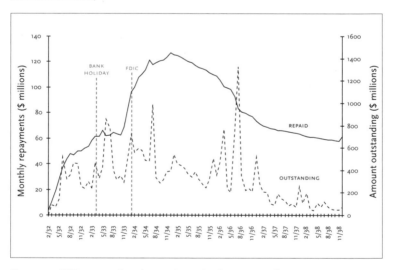

Figure 3.4   RFC repayments and amounts outstanding, 1932–1938   [Source: Report of the Reconstruction Finance Corporation (quarterly), various issues.] [Note: The numbers presented above include repayments and amounts outstanding under the RFC loan and preferred stock programs combined. Only loans to open banks are included. Does not include loans to receivers or those made on preferred stock. Preferred stock includes investments made through notes and debentures to banks in states that prohibited preferred stock investments.]

banks had repurchased nearly $100 million of their preferred stock and capital notes.

At the beginning of 1936, the largest banks retired their preferred stock. By July 1936, the amount of RFC assistance outstanding was down almost 35% from its December 1934 peak. Over half this decline occurred during the six months of January–July 1936, when repayments hit their peak. Morgenthau and Roosevelt were delighted to discover that these repayments contributed $239 million to the fiscal 1936 budget. They were even more delighted when Jones informed them that he could probably net another $700 million in fiscal year 1937 by "slowing down the pace of [RFC] loans and not providing funds to other government agencies."[95]

The recession of 1937 and the growing need to finance war production allowed the RFC to continue providing a wide variety of business finance through 1953, when it was liquidated amid charges of influence peddling and corruption. During hearings in the early 1950s, Hoover and Jones both supported liquidation, feeling that the agency had outlived its usefulness. The liberal practices that became the key to effective government credit programs during the early 1930s were, in the end, a detriment to sound management. Despite bipartisan support for the RFC's liquidation, however, the legacy of its operations lives on through spinoff agencies still in existence today, such as the Federal National Mortgage Association, Export-Import Bank, Commodity Credit Corporation, and Small Business Administration.[96]

SUMMARY AND CONCLUSIONS

During the first six months of RFC operations, the board of directors had a strong sense of purpose, but the powers of the RFC to alleviate the ongoing crisis were diluted by its temporary nature and the conservatism of the reigning administration. Between July 1932 and March 1933, the administration became more active, and powers were expanded, but the board grew disillusioned at the enormity of the task at hand. Only after Roosevelt took office did there exist a strong sense of purpose on the board combined with sufficiently broad powers to offer more than a quick fix for the systemic crisis.

Under the Roosevelt administration, the RFC was used for a variety of purposes beyond lending to the financial and railroad industries.

The Treasury and the Federal Reserve worked closely with the RFC to restore the banking system and guarantee that all banks would join the FDIC in January 1934. By this time, however, RFC assistance to banks had shifted to preferred stock investments more than direct loans, which declined in importance through the rest of the decade (figures 3.3 and 3.4). Furthermore, the RFC under Roosevelt was used to speedily implement New Deal assistance programs of all types without formal appropriations from Congress and was expanded to provide loans for disaster relief, home mortgages, the purchase of electrical appliances (a portion of which subsidized the provision of electrical power to rural locations), agricultural assistance, self-liquidating projects, and foreign trade. By 1935, the preferred stock program had been extended to all industries.

The RFC bank assistance programs, therefore, did not operate in isolation. Many other programs were used to stimulate the economy during the Great Depression, both inside and outside the RFC. Any positive conclusion that can be drawn about bank assistance from the RFC experience has to then be taken jointly with respect to the other programs sponsored by the RFC and the government proper. Current research has not established a beneficial effect of RFC lending to weak banks, although RFC capital assistance — along with changes to management and direct government control — seems to have helped banks back to profitability over a period of five to ten years. Hence, it is difficult to see positive effects arising from current Federal Reserve liquidity facilities, especially lacking the plethora of stimulus programs used by the RFC and other New Deal agencies. Moreover, direct government control over management appears more unpalatable today than it was in the 1930s.

While recapitalization — as with RFC preferred stock — may work, it is unclear whether capital alone plays the primary role in recovery. In the end, it seems the RFC can be considered a "success" in the manner in which it was successfully used to finance tremendous New Deal expansions off the government's balance sheet, though little more.

NOTES

Acknowledgments: I wish to thank Robert Wright, Charles Calomiris, Gary Richardson, Mark Carlson, Eugene White, Larry Neal, the late William Bryan, the Wharton Financial Institutions Center, the Federal Reserve Bank of St. Louis, the editors at SSRC, and the many others who made this research possible.

1 Federal Reserve lending to insolvent institutions is expressly prohibited under Federal Reserve Regulation A.

2 Marvin Goodfriend and Robert G. King, "Financial Deregulation, Monetary Policy, and Central Banking," in *Restructuring Banking and Financial Services in America*, ed. William S. Haraf and Rose Marie Kushmeider (Washington, DC: American Enterprise Institute Press, 1988); and Charles A. E. Goodhart, *The Evolution of Central Banks: A Natural Development?* (London: London School of Economics and Political Science, 1985). See also Michael D. Bordo, "The Lender of Last Resort: Alternative Views and Historical Experience," *Economic Review* (Federal Reserve Bank of Richmond), January/February 1990: 18–28.

3 Mark Carlson and Kris James Mitchener, "Branch Banking, Bank Competition, and Financial Stability," *Journal of Money, Credit, and Banking* 38 (August 2006): 1293–1328; and Elmus Wicker, "A Reconstruction of the Gold and Banking Crises in 1931" (working paper, Indiana University, October 1993), 14.

4 Board of Governors of the Federal Reserve System, *Federal Reserve Bulletin*, September 1937: 907.

5 Milton Friedman and Anna Jacobson Schwartz, *A Monetary History of the United States, 1867–1960* (Princeton, NJ: Princeton University Press, 1963), 308–9; and Wicker, "Reconstruction of Crises," 14.

6 Wicker, "Reconstruction of Crises," 2, 12–15, 29, 33.

7 Wicker, "Reconstruction of Crises," 7; Charles W. Calomiris and Joseph R. Mason, "Contagion and Bank Failures during the Great Depression: The Chicago Banking Panic of June 1932," *American Economic Review* 87, no. 5 (December 1997): 863–84; and Charles W. Calomiris and Joseph R. Mason, "Fundamentals, Panics and Bank Distress During the Depression," *American Economic Review* 93, no. 5 (December 2003): 1615–47.

8 Wicker, "Reconstruction of Crises," 19–22.

9 Wicker, "Reconstruction of Crises," 29–30.

10 Sue C. Patrick, *Reform of the Federal Reserve System in the Early 1930s: The Politics of Money and Banking* (New York: Garland, 1993), 35.

11 Elmus Wicker, *Federal Reserve Monetary Policy, 1917–1933* (New York: Random House, 1966), 173.

12 Friedman and Schwartz, *Monetary History*, 270.

13 Friedman and Schwartz, *Monetary History*, 270. For more on poor management as a cause of banking problems during this era, see David Wheelock and Subal C. Kumbhakar, "The Slack Banker Dances: Deposit Insurance and Risk-Taking in the Banking Collapse of the 1920s," *Explorations in Economic History* 31, no. 3 (July 1994): 357–75; and Milton Esbitt, "Bank Portfolios and Bank Failures During the Great Depression: Chicago," *Journal of Economic History* 46, no. 2 (June 1986): 455–62.

14 Gerald Epstein and Thomas Ferguson, "Monetary Policy, Loan Liquidation, and Industrial Conflict: The Federal Reserve and the Open Market Operations of 1932," *Journal of Economic History* 44, no. 4 (December 1984): 957–83.

15 Negative yields-to-maturity obtained as demand pushed up the prices of government notes and certificates. Par plus interest became less than the sale price of these fixed coupon securities, forcing $\left[\left(I+\frac{M-B_0}{n}\right)\middle/\left(\frac{M+B_0}{2}\right)\right]<0$, where I = interest rate, M = par value, Bo = current sale price, and n = time to maturity. See Lawrence J. Gitman, *Principles of Managerial Finance*, 5th ed. (New York: Harper & Row, 1988), 257.

16 Gerald Epstein and Thomas Ferguson evaluate the impact of these portfolio shifts on various categories of earnings in "Monetary Policy, Loan Liquidation."

17 *Commercial and Financial Chronicle* (William B. Dana Company), February 11, 1933, 936, 939; and Barrie A. Wigmore, *The Crash and its Aftermath: A History of Security Markets in the United States, 1929–1933* (Westport, CT: Greenwood Press, 1985), 356.

18 James Stuart Olson, *Herbert Hoover and the Reconstruction Finance Corporation, 1931–1933* (Ames, IA: Iowa State University Press, 1977), 25.

19 James Stuart Olson, *Saving Capitalism* (Princeton, NJ: Princeton University Press, 1988), 13.

20 Hoover's experience as the head of the Food Administration on the War Industries Board during World War I convinced him that voluntary efforts (such as the wartime victory garden program) could have an effect. For background on inconsistencies in the historical record of Hoover's attitude toward the RFC, see Olson, *Herbert Hoover*, 26, n11. Meyer may have also pushed for the reestablishment of the WFC because he stood to assume the chair of such an organization.

21 Olson, *Herbert Hoover*, 1108. Later, during December 1931, railroads felt the need for a cooperative organization of their own in order to prop up security prices. During this month, the Railroad Credit Corporation (RCC) was established. The RCC was "a contrivance for receiving and lending the proceeds of a temporary freight surcharge on particular commodities." Such loans were authorized only to railroads not currently in receivership, primarily for the purpose of preventing interest defaults. By the time the RCC finished lending in May 1933, it had disbursed over $73 million. Donald Victor Hildebrant, "The Reconstruction Finance Corporation" (master's thesis, Ohio State University, 1951), 5–6.

22 Olson, *Saving Capitalism*, 8; and Friedman and Schwartz, *Monetary History*, 320n.

23 John Miller, "The National Credit Corporation," *Investment Banking* 2 (December 2, 1931): 53–7.

24 For a discussion of similar adverse selection issues in state deposit insurance systems, see Charles W. Calomiris, "Regulation, Industrial Structure, and Instability in U.S. Banking: An Historical Perspective," in *Structural Change in Banking*, ed. Michael Klausner and Lawrence J. White (Homewood, IL: Business One Irwin, 1993). Similar issues arose with the U.S. savings and loan crisis during the 1980s.

25 Olson, *Herbert Hoover*, 29.

26 Olson, *Herbert Hoover*, 29–30; and Olson, *Saving Capitalism*, 10.

27 Olson, Herbert Hoover, 30–32.

28 Lester V. Chandler, *American Monetary Policy, 1928–1941* (New York: Harper & Row, 1971), 129.

29 Chandler, *American Monetary Policy*, 6.

30 Chandler, *American Monetary Policy*, 79, 133–34, 440–50; Wicker, *Federal Reserve Monetary Policy*; and Friedman and Schwartz, *Monetary History*, 413.

31 O. M. Attebury, deputy governor at St. Louis, opined that "conditions in the Eighth District provided no justification for further open market purchases." See Friedman and Schwartz, *Monetary History*, 373n.

32 Chandler, *American Monetary Policy*, 440–50; Epstein and Ferguson, "Monetary Policy, Loan Liquidation," 957–83; Friedman and Schwartz, *Monetary History*, 371, 382; and Patrick, *Reform of Federal Reserve*, 82.

33 Quoted in Friedman and Schwartz, *Monetary History*, 380–85.

34 House Committee on Banking and Currency, *Creation of a Reconstruction Finance Corporation: Hearings on H.R. 5060 and H.R. 5116*, 72nd Cong., 1st sess., December 18, 1931, and January 5–7, 1932, 75–90.

35 Interestingly enough, Sabath was not consulted to help draft the legislation at this time. Furthermore, he missed the first day of the session and only heard of the Reconstruction Finance Corporation bill upon returning. Thus he very nearly missed any opportunity to testify at the hearings, much less affect the final shape of the legislation. See House Committee, *Reconstruction Finance Corporation.*

36 Senate Committee on Banking and Currency, *Creation of a Reconstruction Finance Corporation: Hearings on S. 1,* 72nd Cong., 1st sess., December 18–22, 1931, 161, 163.

37 Senate Committee, *Reconstruction Finance Corporation,* 185.

38 Senate Committee, *Reconstruction Finance Corporation,* 193.

39 House Committee, *Reconstruction Finance Corporation,* 78.

40 Friedman and Schwartz, *Monetary History,* 303, 309; Olson, *Herbert Hoover,* 47–55; and J. F. Ebersole, "One Year of the Reconstruction Finance Corporation," *Quarterly Journal of Economics* 47 (May 1933): 467.

41 Ebersole, "One Year," 467.

42 Ebersole, "One Year," 563–83; F. Cyril James, *The Growth of Chicago Banks* (New York: Harper & Brothers, 1938); and Beryl Wayne Sprinkel, "Economic Consequences of the Operations of the Reconstruction Finance Corporation," *Journal of Business of the University of Chicago* 25, no. 4 (October 1952): 211–24.

43 Although there existed no explicit government guarantee for RFC debt, the large amount of RFC debt held by the U.S. Treasury probably instilled confidence in investors.

44 Of the amount authorized, $200 million was allotted to the Department of Agriculture for crop loans. See Olson, *Herbert Hoover,* 39.

45 Hildebrant, "Reconstruction Finance Corporation," 11.

46 Senate Committee, *Reconstruction Finance Corporation,* 38–41. Upon discussion of the effectiveness of RFC lending, the subject of practices of favoritism in lending or other misappropriations of funds often arises. Thus it is interesting to note here that the act creating the RFC provided that the Secret Service Division of the Treasury Department, with more liberal search and seizure limitations than the local gendarmerie, was in charge of investigating or arresting any person seeking to undermine the organization in any manner applicable under the act.

47 Joseph R. Mason, "Do Lender of Last Resort Policies Matter? The Effects of Reconstruction Finance Corporation Assistance to Banks During the Great Depression," *Journal of Financial Services Research* 20, no. 1 (September 2001): 77–95.

48 James, *Growth of Chicago Banks,* 1044.

49 Olson, *Herbert Hoover*, 47–55; Lynne Pierson Doti and Larry Schweikert, *Banking in the American West: From the Gold Rush to Deregulation* (Norman, Oklahoma: University of Oklahoma Press, 1991), 122; and Reconstruction Finance Corporation, *RFC Circular #4* (Washington, DC, 1932), 8.

50 It is important to realize that during the June 1932 crisis other Chicago banks persuaded Dawes to take this loan in order to avoid a further crisis of confidence should Central Republic liquidate. The other Chicago banks accepted much of the credit risk under the arrangement, leaving little reason to believe that the loan arose out of political favoritism. See Calomiris and Mason, "Contagion and Bank Failures."

51 Patrick, *Reform of Federal Reserve*, 87.

52 Hyo Won Cho, "The Evolution of the Functions of the Reconstruction Finance Corporation: A Study of the Growth and Death of a Federal Lending Agency" (PhD diss., Ohio State University, 1953), 21–28; *Commercial and Financial Chronicle* (William B. Dana Company), August 27, 1932, 1422; and Olson, *Herbert Hoover*, 64–67.

53 A report covering RFC activity for February–July 1932 was not released until December 1932.

54 Olson, *Herbert Hoover*, 57–58; and *Commercial and Financial Chronicle* (William B. Dana Company), August 27, 1932, 1422.

55 Sidney Hyman quotes Meyer as complaining that "there is not a single railroad president that I would hire as a $50-a-week clerk" and that few bank presidents "were qualified to run anything more substantial than a sideshow at a carnival." Sidney Hyman, *Marriner S. Eccles: Private Entrepreneur and Public Servant* (Stanford, CA: Stanford University Graduate School of Business, 1976), 82.

56 Senate Committee, *Reconstruction Finance Corporation*, 6–7; Merlo J. Pusey, *Eugene Meyer* (New York: Knopf, 1974), 221; Jesse Jones and Edward Angly, *Fifty Billion Dollars* (New York: Macmillan, 1951), 529–30; Hyman, *Marriner S. Eccles*, 82; and Cho, "Evolution of the Functions," 22. Bestor, the farm loan commissioner, was said to have been a protégé of Meyer. Olson, *Herbert Hoover*, 40.

57 Three examples of such self-liquidating projects are the Bay Bridge from San Francisco to Oakland, the waterworks system in Pasadena, and the Metropolitan Aqueduct from the Colorado River to Los Angeles.

58 Olson, *Herbert Hoover*, 64–67.

59 Hildebrant, "Reconstruction Finance Corporation," 21–25; Cho, "Evolution of the Functions," 21–28; and Olson, *Herbert Hoover*, 92.

60 Hildebrant, "Reconstruction Finance Corporation," 21–25; Cho, "Evolution of the Functions," 21–28; and Olson, *Herbert Hoover*, 92.

61 Olson, *Herbert Hoover*, 92.

62 Olson, *Herbert Hoover*, 93–94.

63 U.S. Bureau of the Census, *Historical Statistics of the United States, Colonial Times to 1970* (Washington, DC, 1975), 2:1075–78.

64 Roosevelt, elected president in November 1932, was not inaugurated until March 1933. By World War II, this policy had been changed to the current system, wherein the president is inaugurated on January 20.

65 Olson, *Herbert Hoover*, 92; Wigmore, *Crash and its Aftermath; and Commercial and Financial Chronicle* (William B. Dana Company), March 11, 1933, 1481–87, 1670–74.

66 Susan Estabrook Kennedy, *The Banking Crisis of 1933* (Lexington, KY, University Press of Kentucky, 1973), 103–128, 147, 158; Olson, *Herbert Hoover*, 104–5; and Jones and Angly, *Fifty Billion Dollars*, 69–71.

67 Kennedy, *Banking Crisis*, 175–77; and Helen M. Burns, *The American Banking Industry and New Deal Banking Reforms, 1933–1935* (Westport, CT: Greenwood Press, 1974), 47–48.

68 Formerly, the comptroller of the currency appointed receivers to failed national banks in order to carry out custodial duties and protect *investors'* value. Management lost control, and the appointed trustee was responsible for liquidating the bank. A conservator, however, was appointed by the comptroller to conserve assets and regulate withdrawals, protecting *depositors'* claims rather than other, ostensibly more informed, investors. The Emergency Banking Act also provided that banks could be reorganized with a vote of depositors holding 75% or more of the bank's deposits or of two-thirds of the stockholders. The National Bankruptcy Act amendment of 1933 extended the possibility of reorganization to firms in receivership, blurring the distinction between the responsibilities of a receiver and a conservator. Charles J. Woelfel, *The Fitzroy Dearborn Encyclopedia of Banking and Finance*, 10th ed. (Chicago: Fitzroy Dearborn Publishers, 1994), 979, 244.

69 Olson, *Herbert Hoover*, 107. An amendment to the Emergency Banking Act on March 24 empowered the Federal Reserve to lend to non-member banks on the collateral of their time of demand notes until March 3, 1934. Individuals, partnerships, and corporations were allowed to borrow from the Federal Reserve System at the discretion of the reserve banks, secured by direct obligations of the United

States and for periods not exceeding ninety days. The Fed accepted these new powers with a spirit of great reluctance. *Commercial and Financial Chronicle* (William B. Dana Company), February 11, 1933, 1626; and Kennedy, *Banking Crisis*, 198–202. Kennedy notes that the directors of the reserve banks felt that RFC lending powers to non-member banks should be strengthened through liberalized collateral requirements rather than through availability of Fed support. Huey Long espoused a variation on this theme by proposing that the president be empowered to declare all state banks members of the Federal Reserve System. Capital debentures were later authorized for use in cases where the law precluded direct preferred stock investments.

70 *Commercial and Financial Chronicle* (William B. Dana Company), February 11, 1933, 1625–26; and Cho, "Evolution of the Functions," 29–32. For more on the use of RFC voting rights, see Cho, "Evolution of the Functions," 29–34; and Cyril B. Upham and Edwin Lamke, *Closed and Distressed Banks: A Study in Public Administration* (Washington, DC: The Brookings Institution, 1934), 234.

71 Agreement on selecting a new chair was actually a pre-condition of the investment in Continental Illinois. However, the current "directors were not disposed to accept" the RFC's choice. They finally acquiesced after a visit to the chair of the RFC in Washington, Jesse Jones. Additionally, eight other directors were replaced with RFC appointees. It is illustrative to note that Continental was quite weak at the time, and a few weeks later, despite a rather large investment in the firm, the RFC did not intervene in First National Bank of Chicago after the death of its chief executive, Melvin Traylor. Jones and Angly, *Fifty Billion Dollars*, 47–49.

72 Kennedy, *Banking Crisis*, 180. State banking authorities were strongly urged to undertake programs similar to that of the Treasury licensing scheme.

73 Olson, *Saving Capitalism*, 65–66.

74 Taber was a classmate of Roosevelt's from Harvard, while Blaine's appointment served to "reassure Republican Senator Robert LaFollette, Jr., of his status in the New Deal." Olson, *Saving Capitalism*, 52; and Jones and Angly, *Fifty Billion Dollars*, 524–25.

75 Reopenings were not always contingent upon financial soundness alone. Political favor (or disfavor) also had a bearing on such decisions. Susan Estabrook Kennedy describes an instance in which A. P. Giannini of Bank of America appealed directly to Secretary of the Treasury Woodin for licensing. Giannini and the governor of the Federal Reserve Bank of San Francisco had "clashed" in the past, and the gov-

ernor therefore refused to certify the bank as solvent. Kennedy, *Banking Crisis*, 186–87.

76 On March 18 an executive order extended Title II to state banks and their correspondent authorities.

77 Olson, *Saving Capitalism*, 69–70; Kennedy, *Banking Crisis*, 189–91; and Jones and Angly, *Fifty Billion Dollars*, 47.

78 Special provisions were made for purchase notes and debentures of state banks whose laws precluded the issuance of preferred stock. Only in Oklahoma could banks not participate in some aspect of the preferred stock program.

79 Kennedy, *Banking Crisis*, 190–93. See also Upham and Lamke, *Closed and Distressed Banks*, 124–41.

80 Kennedy, *Banking Crisis*, 193–95. In October 1933 the RFC established the Deposit Liquidation Board at Roosevelt's behest in order to provide an orderly liquidation of bank assets nationwide. The board was technically an extension of the executive branch, although it was funded by, and worked very closely with, the RFC.

81 Wigmore, *Crash and its Aftermath*, 468.

82 Jones and Angly, *Fifty Billion Dollars*, 27; Charles W. Calomiris and Eugene N. White, "The Origins of Federal Deposit Insurance," in *The Regulated Economy: A Historical Approach to Political Economy*, ed. Claudia Goldin and Gary D. Libecap (Chicago: University of Chicago Press, 1994), 145–88; and Wheelock and Kumbhakar, "The Slack Banker."

83 Jones and Angly, *Fifty Billion Dollars*, 27.

84 Burns, *American Banking Industry*, 121.

85 Jones and Angly, *Fifty Billion Dollars*, 26–27; Burns, *American Banking Industry*, 123–25; and Wigmore, *Crash and its Aftermath*, 468–70.

86 Olson, *Saving Capitalism*, 79.

87 Jones and Angly, *Fifty Billion Dollars*, 28.

88 Roosevelt appointed Henry Morgenthau Jr. to be secretary of the Treasury when Secretary Woodin resigned for health reasons.

89 Jones and Angly, *Fifty Billion Dollars*, 28–30.

90 Olson, *Saving Capitalism*, 81.

91 Jones and Angly, *Fifty Billion Dollars*.

92 Olson, *Saving Capitalism*, 82.

93 Olson, *Saving Capitalism*, 180.

94 Olson, *Saving Capitalism*, 181.

95 Olson, *Saving Capitalism*, 182.

96 James McGowen, *The Reconstruction Finance Corporation: Some Historical Perspective* (St. Louis: Washington University Center for the Study of American Business, 1977), 3, 11.

CHAPTER FOUR

After the Storm:
The Long-Run Impact of Bank Bailouts

GUILLERMO ROSAS AND NATHAN M. JENSEN

As we write these words, speculation mounts about the possibility that the United States government will need to intervene more forcefully to redress unabated financial distress in the country's banking system, even after having committed $700 billion to prop up banks. The current financial turmoil illustrates the enormous costs of resolving banking crises. In the United States alone, some estimates put the total cost of buying troubled assets, loans to financial firms, and public guarantees at $9 trillion.[1] Yet, there is considerable concern that government-sponsored bailouts will not be entirely effective in stemming the banking crisis, while they will be extremely costly to taxpayers. For example, by December 2008, taxpayers had lost over 50% of the U.S. government's $40 billion investment in AIG.[2] Newspapers in the United Kingdom worry about further banking losses despite £954 billion in government support to the financial sector—an amount equal to £31,800 per taxpayer.[3]

Much of this concern is due to the sheer difficulty of solving systemic problems within the financial sector, yet others are troubled by the use to which bailout money is put. A series of *New York Times* articles documented the misuse of U.S. support to banks. One week after receiving an $85 billion bailout from the U.S. government, AIG executives spent $442,000 on a spa retreat to Monarch Beach, California.[4]

As Bank of America was preparing to pressure U.S. lawmakers for an additional $20 billion in support, CEO John Thain spent $1.2 million to overhaul his personal office, complete with a $1,200 garbage can.[5] One story uncovered the extensive lobbying activity of banks receiving financial support; Citigroup spent $1.77 million in the fourth quarter of 2008 alone on lobbying activities after receiving $45 billion in government support.[6]

These stories generate cynicism about banking policy and provide fodder for late-night comedians, but they also leave considerable room for academic scholarship to systematically evaluate the effectiveness of post-crisis banking policy. In this chapter we focus on the economic impact of government bailouts. In the first section, we briefly discuss existing scholarship on, and provide a descriptive picture of, the economic consequences of banking crises. In the second section, we investigate alternative styles and degrees of government-sponsored "bank bailouts" and generate cross-nationally comparable measures of government support during banking crises. In the third section, we analyze whether the form and generosity of bank bailouts are associated with post-crisis patterns of economic growth, the fiscal cost of intervention, and to a more limited extent, the possibility of distributional shifts in rents and wages accruing to capital and labor.

We confirm previous findings in the literature suggesting that larger bailouts are associated with greater fiscal costs to the state. This should not surprise the reader, as it is obvious that taking on more financial losses from banks can only increase the taxpayers' tab. Yet the hope behind bailouts is that they will help the economy recover faster from a banking crisis through unflinching support of distressed banks. However, we do not find evidence that larger bailouts buffer economies from the negative outcomes of banking crises. Though our results remain tentative, our analysis casts skepticism on the effectiveness of government bank policy, as we fail to find conclusive evidence that larger bailouts are associated with lower declines in economic output or faster rates of economic growth in the aftermath of banking crises or that they ameliorate their distributional costs, as defined by labor's share of national income.

Though we find that costly bailouts fail to provide much reprieve from the negative economic outcomes of banking crises, our conclusions are not entirely gloomy; we also find that political regimes are good predictors of these very same economic outcomes. Consistent with theoretical arguments about the strength of electoral accountability mechanisms,[7] it appears that democracies are less likely to generate extremely onerous bailouts and that they cushion some of the negative economic impact of banking crises. We realize that at a moment in which the two oldest democracies in the world spend billions to prop up distressed banks, this conclusion provides little more beyond the cold comfort of knowing that things could have been much worse under different constitutional arrangements in the United States and Great Britain. Furthermore, this "buffering effect" of democratic regimes does not extend to alleviating the distributional consequences of banking crises, which we define as labor's share of national income.[8] In fact, we find that neither political regimes nor different types of bailout policies are relevant predictors of post-crisis changes in income shares accruing to labor, which we inspect as a proxy of the impact of banking crises on economic distribution.

ECONOMIC CONSEQUENCES OF BANKING CRISES

Banking crises are episodes of widespread insolvency in a country's banking system. Casual readers of financial history will find this story familiar: A fast and excessive build-up of credit feeding the frenzied purchase of assets is abruptly stopped by the sudden burst of a speculative bubble. On the upswing, individuals borrow heavily to acquire appreciating assets in the expectation that they will be able to sell them at a profit in the foreseeable future. On the downswing, asset prices return to values closer to underlying fundamentals, which leaves individuals holding bank debts that are larger than the value of their assets. As asset prices fall, the number of asset owners that stop making payments to their banks increases. Suspecting that an ever-growing share of non-performing loans will affect the financial health of their bank, depositors run for the exits to salvage their savings. Runs on a small number of banks spread to the rest of the banking sector, leading to loss of confidence in the financial health of a wide variety of institutions. Deposits dry up, and lending grinds to a halt.[9] Fulfilling the original fears of depositors, banks become insolvent and either receive government support to continue operations or are allowed to fail.

Throughout the modern era, governments have developed a variety of mechanisms to prevent this type of dynamic from exploding into widespread insolvency in a country's banking system. Deposit insurance, the imposition of bank capital requirements, and Hamilton's Rule[10] (also known as the Thornton-Bagehot lender-of-last-resort doctrine) are some of the tools that help governments prevent some of the dire consequences of asymmetric information in finance. But despite the routine use of these mechanisms, banking crises continue to occur and to impose hefty losses in financial markets.

While the direct impact of banking crises on the banking sector is obvious, it is stunning how banking crises can contribute to broad declines in economic output. Federal Reserve chairman Ben Bernanke has written extensively on banking crises and argues that the Great Depression was partially a result of the credit crisis associated with U.S. banking problems.[11] This "credit channel" affects business activity directly by drying up bank lending during a crisis. Indeed, recent cross-national scholarship has confirmed that banking crises have a severe impact on the availability of credit.[12] This leads to declines in production and employment that have serious consequences for economic growth.[13] Yet, these declines in output are only part of the overall costs of banking crises to society.

Studying banking crises in sixty-six countries starting as early as 1800, Carmen Reinhart and Kenneth Rogoff find similarities in these events over time. Admittedly, banking crises that occurred two centuries ago, when banking systems and government regulation were profoundly different than those in our day and age, may not necessarily hold useful lessons for dealing with modern financial crises. Despite wide disparities in banking regulation in a set of cases that span two hundred years, the authors still find that banking crises follow from similar causes (asset bubbles, credit booms) and that they all generate large costs to governments; in fact, Reinhart and Rogoff portray banking crises as "equal opportunity" threats since they have the potential to affect developed and developing economies alike.[14] These costs include the oft-cited fiscal costs of the bailout itself—which have increased an order of magnitude over the past three decades[15]—along with a number of less obvious costs: Banking crises are often coupled with an increase in government spending, a decrease in tax receipts, and mounting central government debt that rises an average of 86% following the crisis.[16] Furthermore, bank bailouts may create moral hazard, that is, generate the expectation that aggressive lender behavior will be rewarded through socialization of losses in case of financial insolvency. Indeed, the immediate fiscal impact of a bank bailout is only one part of a larger cost to the government.[17]

The weakness of many studies on the economic consequences of banking crises is the difficulty of sorting out the direct impact of a crisis from the impact of other factors that affect economic performance. For example, while the recent banking crisis has been faulted for deepening the U.S. recession, few scholars would say that the crisis is the only cause of the recession. In many cases, a banking crisis is only the trigger of an economic downturn and may be caused by another economic shock that also affects the real economy.[18]

One way to isolate the impact of banking crises is to compare economic recessions that happen in conjunction with a financial crisis (banking or currency) with those that are not accompanied by a crisis. Scholars have estimated that recessions that occur in conjunction with a financial crisis lead to an additional 10% of output losses not seen in recessions unaccompanied by a financial crisis.[19] An alternative way to explore this question is to see if industries that are more dependent on external finance suffer a larger negative impact in economic activity during a banking crisis. Existing research suggests that banking crises have a disproportionately negative impact on sectors dependent on external capital.[20] Both types of studies illustrate how damaging banking crises can be to the overall economy.

To further investigate the relationship between banking crises and economic activity, we turn to data recently collected by Luc Laeven and Fabian Valencia.[21] The Laeven-Valencia data set on which we base our analysis provides both a tally of the starting dates of systemic banking crises, currency crises, and debt crises and an overview of the policies implemented to contain banking crises in a subsample of 42 episodes. In our first illustration, we inspect data from a total of 124 countries from 1970 to 2007. The basic unit of analysis is the country-year, with each country furnishing 37 observations. In table 4.1, we present summary statistics for a number of macroeconomic indicators comparing country-years during the build-up and after banking crises with country-years in normal times. Some clear patterns are evident in these data. First, we

	BANKING CRISIS		NO BANKING CRISIS
	5 YEARS PRIOR	CRISIS YEAR	ALL YEARS
Growth	1.96%	0.61%	3.72%
GDP pc (U.S. dollars, 2000)	3,591	3,074	5,624
Savings (% GDP)	17.55%	13.41%	17.40%
Unemployment	6.87%	8.89%	9.02%
Male	6.60%	8.31%	8.26%
Female	8.2%	10.55%	10.89%
Inflation	40.66%	432.05%	29.62%

Source: Authors based on data from World Bank, *World Development Indicators 2008* (Washington, DC: 2008); and Luc Laeven and Fabian Valencia, "Systemic Banking Crises: A New Database," IMF Working Paper WP/08/224 (Washington, DC: International Monetary Fund, November 2008) for banking crisis years.

Table 4.1   Comparison of crisis country-years and non-crisis country-years

divide all observations into crisis and non-crisis country-years and find their five-year lags; we want to ensure that we are capturing economic indicators at levels prior to, and therefore certain to be unaffected by, a banking crisis. Average measures of economic indicators for crisis country-years appear in column 2, and averages over all remaining non-crisis country-years appear in column 3. We find that average savings rates are very similar between these two groups and that there are only relatively large differences in the levels of per capita GDP (gross domestic product). We also find that in the five-year period preceding a banking crisis, average growth rates are actually lower than in all other country-years (an average of 1.96% compared to 3.72%) but unemployment rates are also much lower on average during the five-year period immediately preceding the occurrence of banking crises (6.87% compared to 9.02%).

Yet, as one would expect, the macroeconomic picture darkens during a crisis. Economic growth drops to a mean of 0.61%, savings rates decline over 4%, and the level of development drops below levels achieved in the period before the crisis. In our sample, consumer price inflation skyrockets to over 400% on average, and unemployment also rises dramatically to almost 9%. Unemployment following banking crises, while affecting both men and women in the labor force, is much larger among women.[22] While the average inflation rate is definitely affected by a handful of outliers and is thus not representative of the path that most countries follow after a banking crisis, we believe this statistic illustrates the economic plight caused by banking crises. We hasten to add that in our empirical analyses in the next sections, we are careful to control for factors that take into account the varying experiences of countries and to access the influence of outliers on our empirical results. While countries have different experiences with banking crises and bailouts, our goal is to analyze the long-term costs of banking bailouts. We feel confident in our ability to provide generalizations by using a series of control variables and limiting the influence of outliers on our results.

What is less obvious than the worsening of conditions during a crisis, and less studied by scholars, is the long-run impact of banking crises on the economic fortunes of countries. In table 4.2, we present the same data on macroeconomic indicators five years before and five years after a crisis episode based on a sample of 111 banking crises.[23] In this sample, we are thus considering average economic performance before and after a banking crisis. The positive story is that the impact of banking crises on economic growth seems to be short-lived. In this smaller sample, countries actually emerged after the banking crisis with higher average levels of economic growth and lower levels of inflation than prior to the crisis. In most cases, levels of economic growth recovered within three years of the crisis.[24] This is not to say that banking crises lead to improved long-run economic performance; our descriptive data should not be taken as a causal claim on the relationship between crisis and performance. Rather, we simply show that negative changes in growth and inflation rates following banking crises tend to be short-lived.

Unfortunately, levels of savings, unemployment, and overall development exhibit a much deeper long-run negative change after banking crises. In table 4.1 we showed the immediate spike in unemployment during a crisis. In particular, the unemployment picture looks even worse five years into a crisis, with unemployment levels persistently higher than during the period prior to the crisis. While these results are based on a much smaller sample of 32 banking crises (due to the unavailability of unemployment measures), we believe that this is a result that merits further consideration.

Similarly, levels of savings as a percentage of GDP do not recover from the dramatic decreases they sustain during banking crises. Savings rates remain almost 3% lower than during the period before the crisis. These results are especially striking in that savings are measured as a percentage of GDP. As we discuss in the next paragraph, countries also have

	BEFORE CRISIS	AFTER CRISIS
Growth	1.96%	4.04%
Log of GDP pc	7.17	7.08
Savings (% GDP)	17.55%	14.62%
Unemployment	6.87%	9.74%
Male	6.60%	9.14%
Female	8.2%	11.22%
Inflation	40.66%	34.04%

Source: Authors based on data from World Bank, *World Development Indicators 2008* (Washington, DC: 2008); and Luc Laeven and Fabian Valencia, "Systemic Banking Crises: A New Database," IMF Working Paper WP/08/224 (Washington, DC: International Monetary Fund, November 2008) for banking crisis years.

Note: The crisis data are for all observations five years before and five years after the banking crisis.

Table 4.2   Effects of a banking crisis

	MEAN	MINIMUM	MAXIMUM
Non-performing loans	34.16%	4.1%	90%
Output loss (% of GDP)	18.96%	0	122.7%
Gross fiscal cost (% of GDP)	14.32%	0	56.8%

Source: Authors based on data from Luc Laeven and Fabian Valencia, "Systemic Banking Crises: A New Database," IMF Working Paper WP/08/224 (Washington, DC: International Monetary Fund, November 2008).

Table 4.3   The depth and cost of banking crises

dramatic decreases in post-crisis levels of development. Thus, while GDP levels decline after banking crises, savings rates must decline at an even faster pace in order to see a drop in savings-to-GDP levels of 3%. Finally, we find that levels of development (log of GDP per capita) do not tend to return to their pre-crisis levels even five years after a banking crisis.

It does not seem exaggerated to report that banking crises usher in a lost decade of development. An alternative way of expressing this fact comes from examining the depth of economic contractions observed to follow banking crises. In table 4.3 we report descriptive statistics for a sample of up to 104 banking crises. Among other measures, this data set reports the largest share of non-performing loans reached during a crisis as well as an estimate of lost output in the three years following a crisis. The banking crises in this sample reached an average level of 34% of non-performing to total loans, and countries suffered average contractions of about one-fifth of their economies. Thus, even after a number of years of healthy rates of post-crisis economic growth, many countries still remain at levels of development below pre-crisis levels.

Aside from changes in aggregate economic outcomes associated with the occurrence of banking crises, we consider finally the possibility that these events may have serious distributive consequences. For starters, the fiscal cost of a banking crisis represents an obvious redistribution of losses from bank shareholders — and sometimes bank depositors and bank debtors — to taxpayers. Beyond these costs, scholars have found that financial crises — that is, banking, currency, and sovereign debt — are associated with a decline in labor's share of income.[25] For example, Emanuele Baldacci, Luiz de Melo, and Gabriela Inchauste explored changes in income inequality and poverty in a dual design, first considering changes in country-level Gini indices and poverty rates in a sample of 65 financial crises and then examining data at the household level from Mexico.[26] They find that financial crises lead to dramatic increases in poverty and, under some conditions, to increases in income inequality.

To gauge some of these distributive consequences, we look at changes in the compensation of manufacturing employees as a percentage of value added in manufacturing.[27] This is an imperfect measure of labor's share of national income, yet it is the standard measure used by scholars due to its more extensive coverage compared to other distributional measures (such as Gini coefficients) and because it is a measure that is broadly comparable across countries. Thus, following convention, we consider this measure to represent the labor share of income of an economy.[28] While the data are spotty for most of the countries in our sample, we do have complete data starting three years prior to and three years following a banking crisis for a total of 18 countries. In figure 4.1, we plot average values of these data for the year of the crisis (Time = 0) and the three years before and after the crisis.

As illustrated in figure 4.1, the average labor share of income was just below 45% before the crisis and immediately dropped 1.5% in the year after the crisis. The 18 countries in the sample saw an overall average drop in the labor share of income from 44% to 40% three years after a crisis. Put another way, while we know that economic output and value added drop considerably during the recessions that accompany banking crises, these data point to a further distributional effect that disproportionately affects labor. These data suggest that a broader array

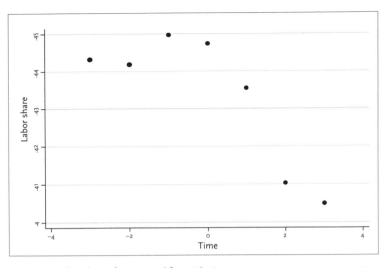

Figure 4.1   Labor share of income and financial crises   [Source: Authors based on data from United Nations Industrial Development Organization, *UNIDO INDSTAT2 2008: Industrial Statistics Database at the 4-digit Level of ISIC (Rev. 2 and 3)* (Vienna: 2008).]

of consequences beyond effects on aggregate outcomes may follow from banking crises.

BANK BAILOUTS IN COMPARATIVE PERSPECTIVE

The doomsday picture of banking crises that we presented in the previous section is not particularly reassuring, either to the concerned public or to policymakers who need to grapple with restoring the banking sector to financial solvency. None of what we have discussed so far tells us whether governments can do anything at all to minimize the real economic consequences of banking crises. Governments are not passive actors fated to absorb all financial losses, but have the capacity and motivation to implement policies to manage banking crises. The main question we attempt to address in this and the next section is whether policy interventions—that is, "bank bailouts"—affect the economic outcomes observed following a banking crisis. Our interest in this question is not normative; we do not seek to argue whether governments should intervene or not to contain and redress banking crises. But these policies are contentious and are often portrayed as efforts to socialize bank losses in bad times without a corresponding attempt to socialize bank profits in good times. Given how contentious these policies are, we would like to know if the degree of intrusiveness or the styles of government responses to banking crises have a discernible association with post-crisis economic outcomes.

In short, we would like to understand if government-sponsored bailouts ease the negative economic effects that follow banking crises. This finding alone would justify sinking large portions of a country's economy in helping to restore financial solvency to banks. Yet, ours turns out to be a difficult endeavor, mostly due to lack of comparable data for a large number of observations. To partially circumvent this problem, we build in this section two different indicators of government response from policy output data in the Laeven-Valencia set referenced previously. In the next section, we use these indicators as predictors of the fiscal costs of crises and the rates of post-crisis economic growth and adjustment in labor share of income.

Though we commonly employ the label "bailout" as if all public interventions to aid banks were identical, governments actually have at their disposal a wide range of policies to counter solvency and liquidity problems in distressed banking sectors. It is common to divide crisis management into containment and resolution policies, depending on whether the purpose is to stop insolvency from spreading into healthier parts of the banking system or to restore banks to a sound financial status. For explanatory purposes, we find it easier to conceive of crisis management policies as belonging to five different issue areas: liability resolution, asset resolution, liquidity support, bank capitalization, and bank exit policy.

Policies in any of these issue areas are directed toward extending the life of distressed banks, that is, banks that are outright insolvent or banks with uncertain solvency status that face liquidity problems. These issue areas mainly affect different parts of the balance sheets of banks. For instance, liability resolution policies alter the structure of bank balance sheets mostly on the debit side of the ledger and include policies such as freezing deposit accounts, enacting bank holidays, extending blanket guarantees that all deposits will be honored, and changing the value of deposits owned by banks (for example, switching the currency denomination of deposits from dollars to pesos). Asset resolution policies alter the credit side of banks' ledgers and include all procedures to remove non-performing loans from balance sheets or to support continuing payments from bank debtors (for example, from mortgage holders in arrears). Similarly, liquidity support, bank capitalization, and bank exit policy aim to prolong the lives of distressed banks by helping them to meet immediate payments from depositors or to keep existing credit lines open, to bolster the capital buffer of banks so they can withstand further losses, and to postpone the denouement of banks that may have run afoul of existing regulatory norms.

We rely on the Laeven-Valencia data set to build two alternative indicators of government response to 42 systemic banking crises that occurred in the period between 1976 and 2007. These 42 cases are a sample of the 124 banking crises for which Laeven and Valencia report data on government response characteristics. The 42 crises in the sample differ from other banking crises in having produced enough information to make their coding relatively easier. As a preliminary step in our analysis, we would like to know whether this implies that these 42 crises are a non-random sample of all 124 crises.[29] To see whether these observations are a representative sample of the larger universe of banking crises, we consider differences in recorded outcomes between crises in the sample and crises not in the sample. Differences in mean values of fiscal cost, output loss, and minimum rate or economic growth achieved following a crisis are not statistically significant. The only significant difference is in the share of non-performing loans, which is on average much larger in out-of-sample crises (42.4%) than in in-sample crises (25.7%). We also know that higher scores on the polity indicator of political regime (see below) and higher per capita GDP increase the probability that a banking crisis will be selected into the sample. It does seem that the banking crises that we do not inspect are characterized by occurring in relatively poorer countries that are less likely to have democratic regimes and more likely to generate larger shares of non-performing loans. We return to this issue of sample selection in the conclusion.

Laeven and Valencia offer several indicators of policies implemented to counter banking crises. We consider a subset of 12 of these indicators that dichotomously code whether a particular policy was enacted or not.[30] Table 4.4 shows the correspondence between these policies and the five issue areas we discussed above. The numbers in the last column of the

ISSUE AREA	POLICY INDICATOR	TIMES ENACTED (MISSING VALUES)
Liquidity support	• Liquidity support/emergency lending	30
	• Lowering of reserve requirements	15 (1)
Liability resolution	• Introduction of deposit freeze	5
	• Introduction of bank holiday	4
	• Blanket guarantee	12
Asset resolution	• Bank restructuring agency	19 (2)
	• Asset management company	25
Bank capitalization	• Recapitalization with public support	32
	• Large-scale government intervention in banks	35
Exit policy	• Regulatory forbearance	28
	• Technically insolvent banks allowed to function	13 (5)
	• Prudential regulations suspended or not fully applied	27 (5)

Source: Authors based on data from Luc Laeven and Fabian Valencia, "Systemic Banking Crises: A New Database," IMF Working Paper WP/08/224 (Washington, DC: International Monetary Fund, November 2008).

Table 4.4   Policy indicators

table correspond to the observed frequency of policy implementation. We can see in this table that some policies are rather popular: almost all governments in the sample opted for large-scale interventions in banks, and almost as many resorted to some scheme of bank recapitalization with public funds. In contrast, very few governments in our sample ever opted to enact deposit freezes or bank holidays.

These twelve policies are indicators of the degree to which governments become involved in containing banking crises. With the exception of some liability resolution procedures, like deposit freezes or bank holidays, most of these policies require public outlays to subsidize distressed banks. Consequently, they have the potential to impose hefty costs on taxpayers.[31] The amount of burden-sharing that governments impose on taxpayers increases to the extent that they implement policies in several of these issue areas at once.

It is not entirely obvious from visual inspection of these data whether governments combine different types of crisis management policies in consistent ways, nor is it clear what trade-offs, if any, governments face in choosing some of these policies over others. One glaring pattern is visible among the few governments that chose to freeze deposits and/or declare bank holidays: these governments did not in general provide blanket deposit guarantees. However, these governments are rather few in number, so it is hard to say whether this indicates a broad regularity in government response.[32] Moreover, we know that at least one combination of policies cannot ever occur because of the system employed to code the information. Thus, whenever a government gets a score of 'o' on regulatory forbearance, it cannot have a score of '1' on either "technically insolvent banks allowed to function" or "prudential regulations suspended."

Because such policy trade-offs might exist in implementing crisis management policies, we believe it is not appropriate to look one by one at the effects of these policies on economic outcomes, such as economic growth, fiscal costs, or changes in the labor share of income. By the same token, building an additive index would confound government responses that may have radically different characteristics. For example, a government enacting only the two bank capitalization policies and a government enacting only the two asset resolution policies would obtain the same score in such an index, without considering the fact that some measures seem to be an almost standard response to banking crises, whereas some others are less frequent. For these reasons, building an index of "government response to banking crises" that simply adds up binary scores is not appropriate.

We seek relatively simple ways of summarizing patterns in these twelve policies, hoping to retrieve a reduced number of meaningful categories or indicators to proxy for different types of government interventions in response to banking crises. We do this in two different ways. Our first approach is essentially inductive and is based on cluster analysis of the twelve indicators in table 4.4. As can be seen in figure 4.2, which is a scatterplot of the two indicators we build, we recognize three government clusters; within each cluster, the "styles" of policy interventions are more or less similar.[33] The smallest group, cluster 2, on the left side of the graph, comprises governments that in response to a banking crisis tended not to lengthen bank exit by engaging in regulatory forbearance but instead tended to rely on the implementation of liability resolution policies. Most of the governments that have enacted bank holidays and deposit freezes are in this cluster, but there are also further similarities among governments in this group: none of these nine governments enacted blanket guarantees or forbearance, suspended prudential regulation, allowed technically insolvent banks to function, or set up a bank

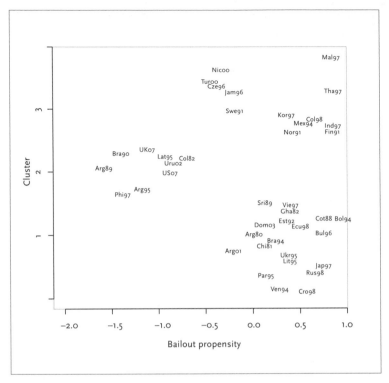

Figure 4.2 Two measures of government-sponsored bailouts [Source: Authors based on data from Luc Laeven and Fabian Valencia, "Systemic Banking Crises: A New Database," IMF Working Paper WP/08/224 (Washington, DC: International Monetary Fund, November 2008).]

restructuring agency. An archetypal "cluster 2" government response would be that of Argentina in 1995, which following the Tequila Crisis lowered reserve requirements and implemented some recapitalization measures but scored '0' on all other policies in the Laeven-Valencia data set.

The other two clusters in figure 4.2 are distinguishable for the policies that they tend to enact rather than for the policies they choose not to implement. The upper cluster (cluster 3) includes countries that tended to provide liquidity support and explicit guarantees and also set up bank restructuring agencies and asset management corporations. These are governments that seemingly took a more direct "hands on" micromanagement approach to the resolution of banking crises. There is however ample variation in the extent to which these governments adhered to firm exit policies; countries in this group were about as equally likely to engage in regulatory forbearance and suspend prudential regulation as to avoid these policies. Finland's response in 1991 combined explicit guarantees, liquidity support, and the establishment of bank restructuring and asset management agencies with suspension of prudential regulations but did not allow insolvent banks to linger long. This contrasts with Korea in 1997, which enacted all these policies but receives a code of '1' for allowing banks to continue functioning despite being technically insolvent.

Finally, governments in cluster 1, the lower cluster, relied heavily on extending the life of insolvent banks through implementation of all three exit policy procedures and for the most part avoided liability resolution policies (see table 4.4). Furthermore, these governments were prone to lowering reserve requirements and were only slightly less likely than governments in cluster 3 to set up bank restructuring and asset management agencies. For example, Russia established an asset management corporation and lowered reserve requirements in 1998, but Ukraine did not carry out any of these policies in 1995; otherwise, these two countries adopted identical policies.

If we were to point out which cluster includes the least intrusive governments, and hence arguably the less profligate spenders, we would point to governments in cluster 2. These countries seem most reluctant to share the burden of bank insolvency with taxpayers; instead, some of these governments have not been shy about impeding depositors from cashing their savings at will. The lower and upper clusters include governments that have enacted multiple crisis management policies, though they differ in the combinations that they have used. These three clusters conform our first categorical indicator of the "style" of government interventions. We expect governments in cluster 2 to generate lower fiscal costs from implementation of crisis management policies; in contrast, governments in clusters 1 and 3 should in principle generate higher fiscal costs but might be more successful in cushioning some of the negative economic impact of banking crises.

One problem with our cluster approach is that it builds categories inductively from sets of countries that seem to "cohere" in some indeterminate, atheoretical way. We consider a second, more principled approach that starts from characterizing each government in the sample as having a latent, unobserved "bailout propensity" that we can infer from its policy choices. To provide a bailout propensity score for each of these governments, we estimate an item-response theory (IRT) model based on the twelve indicators in table 4.4.[34] While a full discussion of an IRT model is technically complicated, the intuition is relatively straightforward. In essence, IRT models allow the estimation of a small number of latent traits to capture variation in a large number of manifest dichotomous indicators. In our context, we can summarize country choices on twelve different banking policies through a unique score on an underlying dimension going from less bailout prone to more bailout prone.

Aside from estimating a bailout propensity score for each government in the sample, we also estimate "difficulty" and "discrimination" coefficients for each of the twelve policy indicators in table 4.4. The difficulty coefficients basically reflect the sample incidence of different policies. For example, liquidity support is a rather popular policy, in the sense that many governments in our sample have turned to it as a measure to alleviate a banking crisis. The fact that the use of this policy is so widespread means that we should not necessarily infer an extremely high bailout propensity from every government that engages in liquidity support. Controlling for the varying "difficulty" of alternative policies provides a more accurate picture of relative bailout propensities. In related fashion, the discrimination coefficients allow us to infer how successful different policies are in helping us separate bailout-prone from bailout-averse governments. For example, in our analyses, "prudential regulations suspended" and "large-scale government intervention in banks" have relatively large and positive discrimination coefficients, suggesting that the enactment of these policies more often than not signals a high bailout propensity. In contrast, "deposit freeze" and "bank holiday" have negative discrimination coefficients, suggesting that these policies are implemented by governments with relatively low bailout propensities (that is, governments that are less willing to pass the costs of insolvency on to taxpayers). In short, estimating difficulty and discrimination coefficients for each of the twelve crisis management indicators is tantamount to recognizing, as we believe is necessary, that these policy indicators differ in the amount of information they reveal about underlying bailout propensities.

Point estimates of the bailout propensities of the 42 governments in our sample are plotted along the horizontal axis of figure 4.2.[35] The IRT model confirms that governments in cluster 2, the ones we consider to be less profligate spenders, have indeed relatively low bailout propensities. However, the IRT model shows little overall difference in the bailout propensities of governments in clusters 1 and 3. One conspicuous difference between our two indicators concerns the placement of five governments: Czech Republic 1996, Jamaica 1996, Nicaragua 2000, Sweden 1991, and Turkey 2000. These would appear to be governments with middling bailout propensities that stand out from the rest of the cases in cluster 3, despite the fact that they all adopted policies that are relatively similar. Be this as it may, we use both the three-way categorical indicator and the continuous bailout propensity indicator in the next section to infer whether more intrusive crisis management (bailout propensities) or different "styles" of government response (clusters) are associated with alternative long-run economic outcomes.

THE ECONOMIC CONSEQUENCES OF BAILOUTS

In this section, we consider the impact of government responses on four economic outcomes: overall fiscal cost of the intervention, amount of lost output, speed of economic recovery (more precisely, softening of the ensuing economic recession), and impact on wage earners. A stronger case for heavy government intervention would require showing that, despite hefty fiscal costs, more intrusive policies are better at cushioning the negative economic consequences of banking crises, all else constant. Our analysis is limited by a relatively small number of observations. Though we have information on bailout propensities and styles for 40 countries (current government responses in the United States and Great Britain are removed), missing data on crucial variables reduces our pool of cases, especially when it comes to labor share statistics.

In our regression models, we attempt to control for other covariates that presumably affect the choice of government response (in that they are causally prior to policy choices) and are also likely to have a direct effect on economic outcomes. The magnitude of financial insolvency of a banking sector prior to implementation of government policies is very likely an important determinant of these four economic outcomes, as well as of the style and depth of government response. Scholars have struggled to construct a measure of insolvency that is distinct from and unaffected by government response. Consider the index of non-performing loans reported by Laeven and Valencia. Though this index could be construed as an indicator of the depth of financial distress in banks, it actually reports the largest share of bad loans reached during the crisis, sometimes after at least some form of government intervention has already occurred. For example, in the context of the current subprime mortgage crisis, the governments of the United States and Great Britain have implemented several measures to prop up banks, and yet it is not certain that non-performing loans have already reached their highest levels. We face the same problem with variables that code the largest "observed deposit drop" in a certain period or the number of banks that are eventually closed.

We address this problem by controlling for the relative importance of the banking sector in a country's economy before the onset of a crisis. This is not a perfect measure of the impact of the crisis, but we believe it provides a good approximation to the size and depth of the financial crisis. We operationalize this by considering the value of bank deposits (deposits) and domestic credit provided by the banking sector (credit), both measured as percentage of GDP during the first pre-crisis year. In fact, the sample correlation between these two measures is 0.83, which provides more evidence that they both reflect the size of the banking sector, if not the magnitude of financial distress. Presumably, the need to protect a country's banking system by implementing massive policy responses is larger where the relative value of deposits and reliance on bank credit are larger.

We also control for the political regime within which governments operate (polity), based on extant evidence that the mechanism of democratic accountability limits the ability of governments to commit to overtly intrusive policies and to shift losses generated from crony relations between bankers and politicians onto taxpayers and also on more limited evidence that democratic regimes suffer banking crises of lower magnitude and frequency than non-democratic regimes.[36] Finally, we include a country's per capita gross domestic product (GDP pc, log scale) as a proxy for its level of economic development, which is in principle associated with bureaucratic capacity and a relative abundance of

	MODEL 1	MODEL 2	MODEL 3
Bailout propensity		0.687**	
		(0.287)	
Bailout Cluster 2			−1.358**
			(0.565)
Bailout Cluster 3			0.138
			(0.516)
Polity 2	−0.089**	−0.067*	−0.067*
	(0.041)	(0.039)	(0.038)
GDP pc (log)	−0.006	−0.016	−0.043
	(0.221)	(0.204)	(0.210)
Deposits to GDP	−0.641	−0.804	−0.613
	(0.601)	(0.558)	(0.593)
Bank credit (log)	0.719*	0.650*	0.588
	(0.396)	(0.367)	(0.390)
Intercept	−4.298**	−4.010**	−3.429*
	(1.745)	(1.614)	(1.763)
N	32	32	32
R^2	0.231	0.370	0.415
(adj. R^2)	(0.117)	(0.249)	(0.275)
F (df)	2.02 (4,27)	3.05 (5,26)	2.96 (6,25)
(p-value)	(0.119)	(0.027)	(0.025)

Source: Authors based on data from Luc Laeven and Fabian Valencia, "Systemic Banking Crises: A New Database," IMF Working Paper WP/08/224 (Washington, DC: International Monetary Fund, November 2008); and World Bank, *World Development Indicators 2008* (Washington, DC: 2008).

Note: * p-value > t = 0.1; ** p-value > t = 0.05

Table 4.5   Models of fiscal cost

resources to combat a banking crisis. This measure is highly correlated with the level of democracy, and we note the implications of this correlation when we discuss the empirical results.

We start by inspecting the effect of bailouts on the gross fiscal cost of intervention. In the Laeven-Valencia sample of crises from 1976–2007, the cost ranges from 0% to 56.8%, with the median banking crisis draining 13% of GDP. Table 4.5 reports estimates from regressions of gross fiscal cost on bailout propensity and cluster while controlling for deposits, credit, GDP pc, and polity. Model 1 presents a baseline model that excludes indices of government intervention and confirms known facts about the tendency of democracies to generate lower fiscal costs; in this model, shifting polity from its minimum to its maximum value while keeping other variables constant at mean sample values leads us to expect a shift in gross fiscal cost from around 7% to 37.2%. Model 1 also suggests that fiscal costs are larger where the banking sector has more relative weight in providing credit.

Models 2 and 3 add, respectively, our bailout propensity and cluster indicators to this basic model. Model 2 confirms that bailout propensity is associated with larger fiscal costs, even after controlling for confounding factors. The estimated size of the effect is not trivial, as it implies that increasing bailout propensity from the 25th to the 75th percentile while holding other variables constant at their sample mean values leads to a corresponding increase in fiscal cost from 8.9% to around 15.8%.[37] Similarly, model 3 suggests that the more restrained governments of cluster 2 enact policies that are, on average, 9.8 percentage points lower than those implemented by governments in clusters 1 and 3.

While our expectations that lower bailout propensities and more contained bailout styles would generate much lower fiscal costs are borne out empirically, we cannot infer that different bailout propensities or styles have much of an effect on other economic outcomes. Admittedly, we have not been able to probe the association between bailouts and all consequential economic variables. For example, we do not consider the speed with which bank lending resumes after a credit crunch, which might be faster where governments opt for more extensive bailouts. Instead, we take a look at measures of aggregate economic activity in the aftermath of a crisis. Table 4.6 displays our "output loss" (models 4 and 5) and "speed of economic recovery" models (models 6 through 9). Output loss is an estimate of the accumulated drop in gross domestic product over the three periods following an economic crisis compared to what would have obtained had the pre-crisis growth trend continued unabated; this indicator is also taken from the Laeven-Valencia data set and averages 20% in the sample. For speed of recovery, we consider alternatively the annual rate of economic growth during the first post-crisis year in models 6 and 7 (this averages -2.7%) and the average rate of economic growth during the first three post-crisis years in models 8 and 9 (which averages 0.97%). Consistent with arguments about the need to engineer massive government-sponsored bailouts in order to limit spillovers from the financial sector to the real economy, we expect bailout propensity to be negatively associated with output loss and positively associated with economic growth. We would also expect governments in clusters 1 and 3 to suffer less grievous output loss and more rapid economic growth.

	MODEL 4	MODEL 5	MODEL 6	MODEL 7	MODEL 8	MODEL 9
DV	output loss	output loss	growth (t+1)	growth (t+1)	growth (t+1 to t+3)	growth (t+1 to t+3)
Bailout propensity	0.083 (0.068)		−1.406 (1.028)		−0.801 (0.604)	
Bailout Cluster 2		0.012 (0.142)		0.251 (1.955)		1.568 (1.154)
Bailout Cluster 3		0.178 (0.123)		−3.821** (1.784)		−1.207 (1.053)
Polity 2	−0.020** (0.009)	−0.023** (0.009)	0.588** (0.139)	0.628** (0.133)	0.261** (0.082)	0.261** (0.078)
GDP pc (log)	0.042 (0.047)	0.023 (0.049)	0.023 (0.730)	0.499 (0.727)	0.118 (0.429)	0.284 (0.429)
Deposits to GDP	−0.179 (0.145)	−0.072 (0.160)	1.649 (2.001)	−0.377 (2.053)	−0.109 (1.176)	−0.797 (1.212)
Bank credit (log)	0.240* (0.119)	0.182 (0.129)	−3.205** (1.313)	−2.104 (1.351)	−1.251 (0.772)	−0.844 (0.797)
Intercept	−0.905* (0.494)	−0.629 (0.543)	5.365 (5.782)	−0.524 (6.100)	3.424 (3.397)	1.012 (3.602)
N	28	28	32	32	32	32
R^2 (adj. R^2)	0.360 (0.214)	0.388 (0.213)	0.534 (0.445)	0.597 (0.500)	0.412 (0.299)	0.486 (0.363)
F (df) (p–value)	2.47 (5,22) (0.064)	2.22 (6,21) (0.082)	5.96 (5,26) (0.001)	6.17 (6,25) (0.001)	3.64 (5,26) (0.013)	3.94 (6,25) (0.007)

Source: Authors based on data from Luc Laeven and Fabian Valencia, "Systemic Banking Crises: A New Database," IMF Working Paper WP/08/224 (Washington, DC: International Monetary Fund, November 2008); and World Bank, *World Development Indicators 2008* (Washington, DC: 2008).

Note: * p-value > t = 0.1; ** p-value > t = 0.05

Table 4.6 Models of output loss and post-crisis economic growth

All the models reported in table 4.6 include the same control variables employed in the fiscal cost models. As was the case before, we find that our indicator of democracy is a consistent predictor of these economic outcomes. Democratic regimes tend to suffer lower output losses and higher economic growth rates in the aftermath of banking crises. As for our pre-crisis measures of the relative size of the banking sector, we find that countries where banks play an important role in the provision of credit are associated with higher output loss and slower economic recovery, but this effect is not always statistically significant. When we turn to the coefficient signs of our bailout indices, we find results that directly contradict our expectations; however, these coefficients do not in general achieve standard levels of statistical significance. The one exception to this pattern of null results appears in model 7, where countries that belong to cluster 3 appear to be more sluggish in their rate of post-crisis economic recovery. Recall from the previous section that these are governments that tend to take a direct role in micro-managing bank portfolios by setting up asset management corporations and bank restructuring agencies. If anything, it would seem that this combination of policies yields large fiscal costs and is associated with an even harsher depression in the immediate aftermath of a banking crisis (there is no difference in three-year average economic growth after the crisis).[38]

In an effort to further control for the magnitude and scope of banking crises as potential predictors of the effectiveness of bank bailouts, we re-estimated models 1 through 9 adding one of two alternative indicators. We first attempted to proxy for the "global" reach of banking crises by adding the 1990 share of world GDP accounted for by all countries that suffered a banking crisis in year t or year t-1, regardless of whether they appear in our sample. For example, Laeven and Valencia report that banking crises started in seven countries in 1998, which adds to seven banking crises that had started in 1997. Consequently, the 1998 score for global reach of banking crises is simply half the sum of the 1990 share of world GDP of these fourteen countries.[39] Alternatively, we included period dummies in our models, distinguishing between crises in the 1980s, the early 1990s (before or in 1995), the late 1990s, and the first decade of the twenty-first century. For the sake of space, we do not discuss these models here (the results appear in appendix 2). In general, however, most of the relevant results we discuss remain unchanged, with the notable exception that political regime is not a statistically significant predictor of output loss whenever we include the period dummies. Furthermore, the sign on the estimated coefficient on our "global reach" variable is intuitive—that is, it suggests a positive association between more global crises and larger fiscal costs, larger output loss, and slower economic growth after a crisis—but is not statistically significant. Finally, only banking crises in the late 1990s seem to be substantively different, as we find that they lead to lower rates of economic growth (models 6 and 7) and to larger fiscal cost.

We finally consider the degree of association between government responses and changes in the share of a country's economic product that accrues to wage earners. We noted before that the index of labor share of income drops drastically three years into a banking crisis. Unfortunately, after excluding governments for which we lack labor share data, our sample is reduced to 19 observations; the paucity of observations for this particular variable affects the precision of our estimates and introduces potential concerns about non-random missing observations producing bias. Indeed, we estimated models similar to those of tables 4.5 and 4.6 based on a smaller set of 18 observations; not only are all coefficients statistically insignificant, but poor goodness of fit statistics suggest that these models are simply not very informative.

Consequently, we only look at the correlation between changes in labor shares and our bailout propensity index.[40] Across these 19 crises, most changes in labor share from year 1 to year 3 were negative, with a mean sample value of about –6.52%, but there are two countries — Latvia and Paraguay, both in 1995 — whose banking crises were followed by large increases in labor share of income.[41] Figure 4.3 plots changes in labor share of income and bailout propensity for nineteen observations with available data. As can be seen from this plot, a pattern emerges only when we disregard the case of the Philippines' response to the East Asian crisis in 1997.[42] Be this as it may, we make no claims that higher bailout propensities lead to distributive outcomes that affect wage earners disproportionately. To be able to make this claim, we would at the very least need to control for confounding covariates in a larger sample and to present a convincing argument that selection of governments into different bailout propensities is more or less random after controlling for those covariates. These are arguments we cannot make at this point.

Our results suggest that bank bailouts yield larger fiscal costs, but we fail to find any such association between bailouts and long-run measures of economic recovery. We stress that this is not conclusive evidence of lack of a causal relationship between bank bailouts and economic performance. Our project is a first step toward understanding this relationship, but much work needs to be done; we believe that scholars across a variety of academic disciplines using diverse methodologies and research designs can best tackle this important question. Yet our results do highlight the lack of clear evidence that bank bailouts exert a positive effect on long-run economic performance. As we mentioned before, it is possible that government bailouts are effective in alleviating credit crunches, an outcome we do not consider here, but if this were so we would probably also see economies recovering faster after intrusive bailouts. If bank bailouts are not clearly effective in helping economies recover from

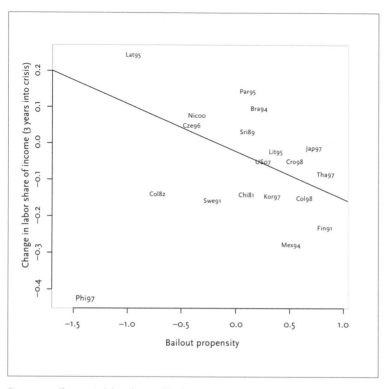

Figure 4.3   Changes in labor share and bailout propensities   [Source: Authors based on data from Luc Laeven and Fabian Valencia, "Systemic Banking Crises: A New Database," IMF Working Paper WP/08/224 (Washington, DC: International Monetary Fund, November 2008); and United Nations Industrial Development Organization, *UNIDO INDSTAT2 2008: Industrial Statistics Database at the 4-digit Level of ISIC (Rev. 2 and 3)* (Vienna: 2008).]

banking crises, why do politicians choose to implement these policies?

We can appeal to different bodies of research that could throw light on this counterintuitive result. First, scholars working on the political economy of trade have long pointed out that trade protection is economically inefficient yet strangely persistent across countries. Arye Hillman's seminal contribution specifically explores why declining industries have the ability to lobby governments for trade protection.[43] The key insight is that firms may have an ability to influence policy through a variety of mechanisms (campaign contributions, lobbying, and so forth) and this power can actually increase when a politically important firm's survival is threatened.

Second, the growing literature on the political economy of the International Monetary Fund (IMF) provides further insights into government responses to banking crises. While scholars have linked IMF programs to lower levels of economic growth, there are important constituencies that benefit from implementation of such programs.[44] For example, James Vreeland shows that IMF programs lead to a redistribution from labor to capital similar to the one suggested by our preliminary results on bank bailouts.[45] One reason why citizens tolerate IMF programs despite these negative distributional consequences is that rejecting IMF support entails very high costs, including further deepening of a financial crisis. This deepening occurs because rejection of an IMF program sends a negative signal to international investors that the government is not willing to engage in serious reform. A similar dynamic could explain public tolerance of bank bailouts. Bailouts may have distributional consequences, but citizens and politicians alike may perceive that the risks associated with doing nothing are enormous.

Third, a common thread in discussions about government responses to banking crises, especially following the East Asian debacle of 1998, is to blame bank bailouts on crony capitalism. In this view, it would hardly be surprising that bailouts are ineffective as they are not really meant to salvage the economy but rather to subsidize the losses of politically connected bank shareholders. Blaming bailouts solely on crony relations between politicians and bankers makes for a rather simplistic explanation, though, as it fails to account for the wide variation in policies that make up government responses to banking crises. Furthermore, crony links would force politicians to implement bailouts only if they are unconstrained by other links of representation. Indeed, theoretical accounts about the salutary effects of democratic regimes are ultimately premised on the possibility that electoral accountability may trump what might otherwise be extreme pressure from bankers on politicians to transfer losses to taxpayers.

Our final conjecture concerns uncertainty about policy effects. Not only is there little agreement within the academic and policy communities about the kind of policies that work in different situations, but even the most "consensual" views seem to have changed across different historical periods, as Charles Calomiris has noted recently.[46] That uncertainty about which policies are likely to work is not surprising. Politicians lack the luxury of policy experimentation during banking crises. They do have recourse to history, but the lessons they can extract are constrained by the same problems that affect the ability of scholars to learn from observational data. And to make matters worse, politicians act in an environment of asymmetric information about the true financial status of banks, with little time to ponder the likely impact of different policies.

CONCLUSION

In this chapter we have explored how post-crisis banking policy affects the costs of bailouts and the speed of economic recovery following a banking crisis. By analyzing a number of banking crises and associated government interventions, we find that while extensive bank bailouts are financially costly, we cannot substantiate that they actually alleviate the long-run impact of banking crises on output declines, growth, and redistribution from labor to capital following a crisis. If anything, our coefficient estimates are signed in a direction that suggests that more intrusive bank bailouts lead to larger output loss, less rapid economic recovery, and worse distributive outcomes from the point of view of wage earners.

However, two reasons remain that prevent us from interpreting our results as an indictment against bank bailouts. The first reason has to do with the kinds of outcomes that we have inspected. Some accounts from the recent failure of Lehman Brothers suggest that allowing financial intermediaries to collapse may have dire consequences, especially in suddenly freezing credit markets. Indeed, the notion of systemic risk, that is, the possibility that the collapse of a single financial intermediary could spread distress across a larger number of banks, is one with which policymakers are well acquainted. Against this possibility, many of the policy interventions that we have analyzed are used to contain the crisis and to "thaw" frozen credit lines among banks and between banks and firms in other economic sectors. Our analysis examines the long-run impact of these crises and evaluates government support to the banking sector solely based on fiscal costs, output loss, economic growth, and to a more limited extent, the distribution of income between capital and labor. It is entirely possible that bank bailouts have some positive effects in the short run — containing financial distress, restoring confidence in the banking system, stopping credit crunches — that justify their enormous costs. And still, bank bailouts are also likely to generate other unmeasured negative consequences, such as rent-seeking and moral hazard problems.

The second reason concerns the difficulty of arriving at solid causal inferences from observational data. We consider two problems here. First, the sample of banking crises for which we have government response data does not seem to reflect the characteristics of the entire population of 124 banking crises in the Laeven-Valencia set. As we mentioned before, the instances of government response that we inspected were more likely to have occurred in slightly richer, more democratic polities and to generate lower shares of non-performing loans at the peak of the crisis. If we were to interpret our estimates of the impact of political regimes on long-run economic outcomes as causal effects, we would need to conclude that the out-of-sample banking crises probably generated even poorer economic results. Furthermore, previous findings confirm that democratic regimes are less likely to implement extensive bailouts. Again, the higher incidence of non-democracies among out-of-sample banking crises leads us to expect government responses that approximate the higher end of bailout propensity. Even here, words of caution are necessary. Though we have strong theoretical reasons to expect that politicians in democratic regimes will choose more contained bailouts and will limit fiscal costs, we do not have similarly sound prior expectations about the effect of political regimes on economic recovery or distributional outcomes. We would also need to consider the potential association between political regimes, on the one hand, and economic recovery and distributional outcomes, on the other, after controlling for factors that may be systematically different across political regimes and that may have a direct impact on those two variables. Such is the case of institutional configurations concerning capital openness and exchange rate regimes.[47]

The second and more pressing problem in our search for the effects of bank bailouts concerns non-random assignment of government response. We consider that governments have latitude in choosing policies to deal with bank insolvency and illiquidity during a banking crisis. We also acknowledge that banking crises vary in their magnitude and scope. Despite our best efforts to construct a valid indicator, we have not been able to control for the magnitude of banking crises prior to any kind of government intervention. It stands to reason that magnitude drives response, at least partially, and should also have an effect on economic outcomes. We tried to palliate this problem by controlling for the relative importance of the banking sector in a country's economy, but we still consider that future work ought to revisit the issue of causality either by building appropriate indicators of magnitude of the crisis prior to policy response or by developing more creative research designs.

NOTES

Acknowledgments: Thanks to Bob Colvin for excellent research assistance and to the Murray Weidenbaum Center on the Economy, Government, and Public Policy at Washington University in St. Louis, which provided funding for data collection. We also appreciate comments from the editors of this volume and from anonymous reviewers. We are solely responsible for any remaining errors.

1   Liz Moyer, "A TARP in the Trillions?" *Forbes.com,* January 21, 2009, http://www. forbes.com/2009/01/21/tarp-banking-treasury-biz-wall-cx_lm_0121tarp.html.

2   Edmund L. Andrews, "No easy answers as Obama team faces banking crisis," *International Herald Tribune,* January 21, 2009.

3   Gordon Rayner, "Financial Crisis: Just how big is Britain's toxic debt?" *Telegraph,* January 23, 2009.

4   Michael J. de la Merced and Sharon Otterman, "A.I.G. Takes Its Session in Hot Seat," *New York Times,* October 7, 2008.

5   Andrew Ross Sorkin, "Thain's Office Overhaul Said to Cost $1.2 Million," Deal-Book Blog, *New York Times.com,* January 22, 2009, http://dealbook.blogs.nytimes. com/2009/01/22/thains-office-overhaul-said-to-cost-12-million/.

6   David D. Kirkpatrick and Charlie Savage, "Firms That Got Bailout Money Keep Lobbying," *New York Times,* January 23, 2009.

7   Guillermo Rosas, *Curbing Bailouts: Bank Crises and Democratic Accountability in Comparative Perspective* (Ann Arbor: University of Michigan Press, 2009).

8   In future research we hope to explore other distributional impacts of banking crises and government responses to these crises, including impacts on income inequality, levels of poverty, and ratio of men's to women's income.

9   See Graciela L. Kaminsky and Carmen M. Reinhart, "The Twin Crises: The Causes of Banking and Balance-of-Payment Problems," *American Economic Review* 89, no. 3 (June 1999): 473–500; and Michael Bordo et al., "Is the crisis problem growing more severe?" *Economic Policy* 16, no. 32 (April 2001): 52–82. For a less pessimistic

view of the impact of banking crises on deposits and lending, see Asli Demirgüç-Kunt, Enrica Detragiache, and Poonam Gupta, "Inside the crisis: An empirical analysis of banking systems in distress," *Journal of International Money and Finance* 25, no. 5 (2006): 702–18.

10 Richard Sylla, Robert E. Wright, and David J. Cowen, "Alexander Hamilton, Central Banker: Crisis Management during the U.S. Financial Panic of 1792," *Business History Review* 83, no. 1 (Spring 2009). See also Robert F. Wright, *One Nation Under Debt: Hamilton, Jefferson, and the History of What We Owe* (New York: McGraw-Hill, 2008), 157–60.

11 Ben S. Bernanke, "Non-Monetary Effects of the Financial Crisis in the Propagation of the Great Depression," *American Economic Review* 73, no. 3 (June 1983): 257–76.

12 For a review, see Ben S. Bernanke and Mark Gertler, "Inside the Black Box: The Credit Channel of Monetary Policy Transmission," *Journal of Economic Perspectives* 9, no. 4 (Fall 1995): 27–48.

13 For a review of the literature and data sources, as well as original data analyses, see Edward J. Frydl, "The Length and Cost of Banking Crises," IMF Working Paper WP/99/30 (Washington, DC: International Monetary Fund, March 1999); and Barry Eichengreen and Carlos Arteta, "Banking Crises in Emerging Markets: Presumptions and Evidence," in *Financial Policies in Emerging Markets*, ed. Mario I. Blejer and Marko Škreb (Cambridge, MA: MIT Press, 2002).

14 Carmen M. Reinhart and Kenneth S. Rogoff, "Banking Crisis: An Equal Opportunity Menace," NBER Working Paper No. 14587 (Cambridge, MA: National Bureau of Economic Research, December 2008).

15 Charles W. Calomiris, "Banking Crises," *NBER Reporter* 4 (2008): 10–14.

16 These banking crises are also associated with sovereign defaults on external government debt. Reinhart and Rogoff, "Banking Crisis."

17 The costs of a banking crisis can also be understated by only looking at the short-run drop in output. See John H. Boyd, Sungkyu Kwak, and Bruce Smith, "The Real Output Losses Associated with Modern Banking Crises," *Journal of Money, Credit, and Banking* 37, no. 6 (December 2005): 977–99.

18 For a very recent discussion, see Jannett Highfill, "The Economic Crisis as of December 2008: *The Global Economy Journal* Weighs In," *Global Economy Journal* 8, no. 4 (2008).

19 Bordo et al., "Is the crisis problem." Glenn Hoggarth, Ricardo Reis, and Victoria Saporta examine the output declines of neighboring countries in "Costs of banking system instability: some empirical evidence," Bank of England Working Paper 144 (London: Bank of England, 2001). They find that countries with banking crises

have a larger impact on output declines than that of their geographic neighbors.

20 Giovanni Dell'Ariccia, Enrica Detragiache, and Raghuram Rajan, in "The real effect of banking crises," *Journal of Financial Intermediation* 17, no. 1 (January 2008): 89–112, find that sectors dependent on external capital have a larger decline in output. They also find that countries that are more dependent on their own banking sectors for capital (having little access to international financial resources) are disproportionately affected by domestic banking crises.

21 Luc Laeven and Fabian Valencia, "Systemic Banking Crises: A New Database," IMF Working Paper WP/08/224 (Washington, DC: International Monetary Fund, November 2008). This data set extends information on banking crises collected by Gerard Caprio, Daniela Klingebiel, Luc Laeven, and Guillermo Noguera in "Appendix: Banking Crisis Database" in *Systemic Financial Crises: Containment and Resolution*, ed. Patrick Honohan and Luc Laeven (Cambridge: Cambridge University Press, 2005), 309–40.

22 Interestingly, the current financial crisis in the United States seems to affect men disproportionately. See Floyd Norris, "In This Recession, More Men Are Losing Jobs," *New York Times*, March 13, 2009.

23 Laeven and Valencia count a total of 124 banking crises in the period from 1976 to 2007, but we lose some of this information because of missing data among our economic indicators.

24 This is consistent with the empirical results of Kaminsky and Reinhardt, "The Twin Crises," and Demirgüç-Kunt, Detragiache, and Gupta, "Inside the crisis."

25 For a recent example, see Ishac Diwan, "Debt as Sweat: Labor, Financial Crisis, and the Globalization of Capital" (working paper, World Bank, 2001). For a broader study on the relationship between capital account openness and distributional issues, see Arjun Jayadev, "Capital account openness and the labour share of income," *Cambridge Journal of Economics* 31, no. 3 (2007): 423–43.

26 Emanuele Baldacci, Luiz de Melo, and Gabriela Inchauste, "Financial Crisis, Poverty, and Income Distribution," IMF Working Paper WP/02/4 (Washington, DC: International Monetary Fund, January 2002).

27 The United Nations Industrial Development Organization (UNIDO) compiles this series in its INDSTAT4 2008 database.

28 James Raymond Vreeland, *The IMF and Economic Development* (New York: Cambridge University Press, 2003).

29 Missing values on crisis outcome variables—non-performing loans, fiscal cost, and output loss—are common in the non-sample crises but not in the sample crises.

30 The 42 governments in the sample are listed in appendix 1 (current government

responses in the United States and Great Britain excluded). Though other policy indicators in the database are coded as continuous variables, it is not always easy to standardize them for the purpose of comparison. Many policies, for example, are coded in a two-step procedure: a dichotomous indicator codes whether the policy is observed or not; if the policy is observed, then a continuous measure is provided. Aside from the difficulty in standardizing these measures, we prefer to rely on the dichotomous indicators because the difference between implementing a policy or not is arguably more important than any differences in size within the set of governments that did implement a particular policy.

31 Deposit freezes affect depositors, who are presumably taxpayers, but this is not a cost that they suffer from subsidizing the losses of some other economic actor.

32 These governments are Argentina 1989 and 2001, Brazil 1990, Ecuador 1998, and Uruguay 2002. With the exception of Brazil, all governments were legally committed to provide some form of deposit insurance, but it is doubtful that this feature alone explains their policy choices.

33 To build the clusters, we compute the squared distance between the policy vectors of all possible pairs of governments in the sample and then use Ward's minimum variance criterion to cluster the less distant pairs together. The plots are slightly jittered for ease of representation.

34 For a detailed explanation of this technique, see Rosas, *Curbing Bailouts*.

35 All details of model estimation are available from the authors.

36 See Philip Keefer, "Elections, Special Interests, and Financial Crisis," *International Organization* 61, no. 3 (July 2007): 607–41; Rosas, *Curbing Bailouts*; and Guillermo Rosas, "Bagehot or Bailout? An Analysis of Government Responses to Banking Crises," *American Journal of Political Science* 50, no. 1 (2006): 175–91. In these pieces, the effect of democratic regimes on fiscal costs and choice of policy response is substantiated even after controlling for potential confounders (such as level of development, capital openness, or central bank autonomy), employing matching procedures to balance political regimes across cases, and using a variety of modeling techniques to bolster a causal account of this effect.

37 This range of variation corresponds to slightly less than half the sample standard deviation of gross fiscal cost.

38 Though we had a strong theoretical rationale to expect that democratic regimes would affect *policy choice* and *fiscal cost* in the previous models, we are not entirely persuaded that political regimes should also affect the speed of recovery. In alternative specifications, we thus omitted *polity* and found that the estimated effect of *bailout propensity* on output loss and economic recovery is still contrary to our expec-

tations and suggests a substantively important impact. We conclude from these alternative specifications that, in the best case, more intrusive bailouts have no effect on economic output or economic recovery in the aftermath of banking crises and, in the worst case, they may actually be associated with even worse economic outcomes.

39 GDP shares are from Angus Maddison, *Historical Statistics for the World Economy: 1–2003 AD* (Paris: OECD Development Centre, 2003), http://www.ggdc.net/maddison.

40 The average changes in labor shares (and standard deviations) within each of the three different clusters are 0.007 (0.095), −0.092 (0.276), and −0.115 (0.125), with 7, 4, and 8 cases, respectively, in each of these groups. Differences among these averages are not statistically significant.

41 24.6% and 14.4%, respectively.

42 In fact, this observation is a very influential outlier in a regression model of changes in labor share on bailout propensity. The Cook's distance statistic for Philippines 1997 is 2.424, which is about 44 times larger than the average Cook's distance for all other observations (0.054). This is a discrepant and highly influential observation. When we exclude this discrepant observation from the sample, the correlation between changes in labor share and bailout propensities is −0.5 (the regression line based on a sample that excludes the Philippines is also plotted in figure 4.3).

43 Arye L. Hillman, "Declining Industries and Political-Support Protectionist Motives," *American Economic Review* 72, no. 5 (December 1982): 1180–87.

44 For a review, see Martin C. Steinwand and Randall W. Stone, "The International Monetary Fund: A Review of the Recent Evidence," *Review of International Organizations* 3, no. 2 (June 2008): 123–50.

45 Vreeland, *IMF and Economic Development.*

46 Calomiris, "Banking Crises."

47 A rather robust empirical finding ties democracies to floating exchange rate regimes, which in principle allow governments more flexibility at the time of committing resources to prop up ailing banking systems; see *inter alia* Michael Hall, "Democracy and Floating Exchange Rates," *International Political Science Review* 29, no. 1 (January 2008): 73–98; and David A. Leblang, "Domestic Political Institutions and Exchange Rate Commitments in the Developing World," *International Studies Quarterly* 43, no. 4 (December 1999): 599–620. For this reason, it is possible that the negative association between democratic regimes and bank bailouts reported in other studies has been underestimated; we still cannot anticipate the direction of bias, if any, that results from failure to control for exchange rate configurations in our long-run economic consequences models.

APPENDIX 1: BANKING CRISES IN SAMPLE

Argentina 1980

Argentina 1989

Argentina 1995

Argentina 2001

Bolivia 1994

Brazil 1990

Brazil 1994

Bulgaria 1996

Chile 1981

Colombia 1982

Colombia 1998

Côte d'Ivoire 1988

Croatia 1998

Czech Republic 1996

Dominican Republic 2003

Ecuador 1998

Estonia 1992

Finland 1991

Ghana 1982

Indonesia 1997

Jamaica 1996

Japan 1997

Korea 1997

Latvia 1995

Lithuania 1995

Malaysia 1997

Mexico 1994

Nicaragua 2000

Norway 1991

Paraguay 1995

Philippines 1997

Russia 1998

Sri Lanka 1989

Sweden 1991

Thailand 1997

Turkey 2000

Ukraine 1995

Uruguay 2002

Venezuela 1994

Vietnam 1997

APPENDIX 2: MODELS OF ECONOMIC CONSEQUENCES UNDER ALTERNATIVE INDICATORS

	MODEL 1	MODEL 2	MODEL 3
Bailout propensity		0.681** (0.296)	
Bailout Cluster 2			−1.355** (0.572)
Bailout Cluster 3			0.169 (0.524)
Polity 2	−0.091** (0.042)	−0.068 (0.040)	−0.069* (0.039)
GDP pc (log)	0.010 (0.227)	−0.011 (0.210)	−0.027 (0.214)
Deposits to GDP	−0.623 (0.611)	−0.797 (0.571)	−0.576 (0.603)
Bank credit (log)	0.681 (0.410)	0.640 (0.380)	0.531 (0.405)
Global reach of crisis	0.028 (0.060)	0.008 (0.056)	0.035 (0.055)
Intercept	−4.404** (1.784)	−4.044** (1.661)	−3.511** (1.788)
N	32	32	32
R^2 (adj. R^2)	0.237 (0.091)	0.370 (0.219)	0.425 (0.257)
F (df) (p–value)	1.62 (5,26) (0.191)	2.45 (6,25) (0.053)	2.54 (7,24) (0.042)

Source: Authors based on data from Luc Laeven and Fabian Valencia, "Systemic Banking Crises: A New Database," IMF Working Paper WP/08/224 (Washington, DC: International Monetary Fund, November 2008); and World Bank, *World Development Indicators 2008* (Washington, DC: 2008).

Note: * p-value > t = 0.1; ** p-value > t = 0.05 .

Table 4.7   Models of fiscal cost (using a "global reach of crisis" predictor)

	MODEL 4	MODEL 5	MODEL 6	MODEL 7	MODEL 8	MODEL 9
DV	output loss	output loss	growth (t+1)	growth (t+1)	growth (t+1 to t+3)	growth (t+1 to t+3)
Bailout propensity	0.076 (0.070)		−1.287 (1.050)		−0.906 (0.609)	
Bailout Cluster 2		0.015 (0.143)		0.232 (1.934)		1.575 (1.164)
Bailout Cluster 3		0.182 (0.124)		−4.023* (1.773)		−1.133 (1.067)
Polity 2	−0.022** (0.010)	−0.024** (0.010)	0.601** (0.142)	0.645** (0.132)	0.249** (0.082)	0.255** (0.079)
GDP pc (log)	0.047 (0.048)	0.029 (0.050)	−0.059 (0.746)	0.396 (0.724)	0.191 (0.432)	0.321 (0.436)
Deposits to GDP	−0.179 (0.147)	−0.070 (0.162)	1.528 (2.026)	−0.615 (2.040)	−0.001 (1.174)	−0.710 (1.228)
Bank credit (log)	0.238* (0.121)	0.175 (0.129)	−3.024** (1.349)	−1.734 (1.369)	−1.413* (0.782)	−0.979 (0.824)
Global reach of crisis	0.007 (0.076)	0.011 (0.013)	−0.145 (0.201)	−0.229 (0.185)	0.129 (0.116)	0.084 (0.111)
Intercept	−0.960* (0.512)	−0.690 (0.552)	5.957 (5.892)	0.009 (6.051)	2.896 (3.415)	0.817 (3.643)
N	28	28	32	32	32	32
R^2 (adj. R^2)	0.369 (0.189)	0.408 (0.200)	0.544 (0.434)	0.621 (0.511)	0.440 (0.305)	0.498 (0.352)
F (df) (p–value)	2.05 (6,21) (0.104)	1.97 (7,20) (0.112)	4.96 (6,25) (0.002)	5.62 (7,24) (0.001)	3.27 (6,25) (0.016)	3.40 (7,24) (0.012)

Source: Authors based on data from Luc Laeven and Fabian Valencia, "Systemic Banking Crises: A New Database," IMF Working Paper WP/08/224 (Washington, DC: International Monetary Fund, November 2008); and World Bank, *World Development Indicators 2008* (Washington, DC: 2008).

Note. * p-value > t = 0.1; ** p-value > t = 0.05

Table 4.8   Models of output loss and post-crisis economic growth (using a "global reach of crisis" predictor)

	MODEL 1	MODEL 2	MODEL 3
Bailout propensity		0.707**	
		(0.266)	
Bailout Cluster 2			−1.406**
			(0.487)
Bailout Cluster 3			−0.738
			(0.558)
Polity 2	−0.092**	−0.054	−0.066
	(0.042)	(0.040)	(0.040)
GDP pc (log)	0.250	0.291	0.362
	(0.219)	(0.196)	(0.219)
Deposits to GDP	−0.743	−0.761	−1.082*
	(0.543)	(0.485)	(0.559)
Bank credit (log)	0.141	0.001	0.216
	(0.403)	(0.364)	(0.369)
Early 1990s	−0.287	−0.851	−0.449
	(0.669)	(0.634)	(0.635)
Late 1990s	1.277*	0.664	1.258*
	(0.634)	(0.611)	(0.693)
Early 2000s	1.424	1.288	1.518
	(0.928)	(0.831)	(1.034)
Intercept	−4.361**	−3.918**	−4.894**
	(1.547)	(1.392)	(1.714)
N	32	32	32
R^2	0.479	0.602	0.625
(adj. R^2)	(0.328)	(0.463)	(0.472)
F (df)	3.16 (7,24)	4.34 (8,23)	4.08 (9,22)
(p−value)	(0.016)	(0.003)	(0.003)

Source: Authors based on data from Luc Laeven and Fabian Valencia, "Systemic Banking Crises: A New Database," IMF Working Paper WP/08/224 (Washington, DC: International Monetary Fund, November 2008); and World Bank, *World Development Indicators 2008* (Washington, DC: 2008).

Note: * p−value > t = 0.1; ** p−value > t = 0.05

Table 4.9   Models of fiscal cost (using period dummies)

	MODEL 4	MODEL 5	MODEL 6	MODEL 7	MODEL 8	MODEL 9
DV	output loss	output loss	growth (t+1)	growth (t+1)	growth (t+1 to t+3)	growth (t+1 to t+3)
Bailout propensity	0.059 (0.075)		−0.869 (0.958)		−0.616 (0.661)	
Bailout Cluster 2		−0.010 (0.139)		0.221 (1.818)		1.536 (1.211)
Bailout Cluster 3		0.242 (0.149)		−1.338* (2.085)		−0.462 (1.389)
Polity 2	−0.078 (0.011)	−0.015 (0.011)	0.646** (0.144)	0.662** (0.149)	0.298** (0.099)	0.279** (0.099)
GDP pc (log)	0.068 (0.053)	0.020 (0.059)	−0.740 (0.706)	−0.430 (0.821)	−0.122 (0.487)	0.034 (0.547)
Deposits to GDP	−0.220 (0.147)	−0.075 (0.169)	2.118 (1.748)	1.399 (2.087)	0.028 (1.205)	−0.272 (1.390)
Bank credit (log)	0.207* (0.125)	0.151 (0.127)	−1.476 (1.309)	−1.400 (1.379)	−0.726 (0.903)	−0.704 (0.919)
Early 1990s	−0.106 (0.171)	−0.158 (0.169)	−0.058 (2.283)	−0.155 (2.369)	−0.457 (1.574)	−0.276 (1.578)
Late 1990s	0.105 (0.166)	−0.020 (0.181)	−5.282** (2.202)	−4.940* (2.589)	−1.915 (1.518)	−1.476 (1.725)
Early 2000s	−0.130 (0.221)	−0.404 (0.272)	−4.989 (2.993)	−3.472 (3.860)	−2.558 (2.064)	−1.298 (2.572)
Intercept	−0.951* (0.494)	−0.444 (0.580)	6.071 (5.013)	3.890 (6.400)	3.943 (3.457)	2.463 (4.264)
N	28	28	32	32	32	32
R² (adj. R²)	0.454 (0.224)	0.514 (0.271)	0.703 (0.560)	0.699 (0.576)	0.483 (0.304)	0.512 (0.312)
F (df) (p–value)	1.98 (8,19) (0.107)	2.12 (9,18) (0.084)	6.80 (8,23) (0.000)	5.68 (9,22) (0.000)	2.69 (8,23) (0.030)	2.56 (9,22) (0.035)

Source: Authors based on data from Luc Laeven and Fabian Valencia, "Systemic Banking Crises: A New Database," IMF Working Paper WP/08/224 (Washington, DC: International Monetary Fund, November 2008); and World Bank, *World Development Indicators 2008* (Washington, DC: 2008).

Note: * p-value > t = 0.1; ** p-value > t = 0.05

Table 4.10   Models of output loss and post-crisis economic growth (using period dummies)

Contributors

BENTON E. GUP is a professor of finance and holder of the Robert Hunt Cochrane/Alabama Bankers Chair of Banking at the University of Alabama's Culverhouse College of Commerce. An expert on banking and financial systems, he has published or edited twenty-eight books and contributed to dozens of others. A former economist with the Federal Reserve Bank of Cleveland, he is author of *Too Big to Fail: Policies and Practices in Government Bailouts*.

NATHAN M. JENSEN is an associate professor in the Department of Political Science at Washington University in St. Louis and a fellow at the university's Center in Political Economy. He teaches courses and conducts research on international financial markets, multinational corporations and development, political risk in emerging markets, trade policy, international institutions, and civil conflict.

JOSEPH R. MASON is an associate professor in the Department of Finance at Louisiana State University, holder of LSU's Hermann Moyse Jr./Louisiana Bankers Association Endowed Chair of Banking, and a senior fellow at the Wharton School. An expert in issues of bank and financial market regulation, as well as responses to bankruptcy and financial crisis, he is the author of a number of works on financial regulation and recovery and has consulted for a wide range of research institutions, government agencies, and corporations.

GUILLERMO ROSAS is an assistant professor in the Department of Political Science at Washington University in St. Louis and a fellow at the university's Center in Political Economy. His research interests include comparative political economy and legislative politics in Latin America. He teaches courses on Latin American politics, political economy of development, and research methods.

ROBERT E. WRIGHT is holder of the Nef Family Chair of Political Economy at Augustana College, a research economist at the National Bureau of Economic Research, editor of Pickering and Chatto of London's financial history monograph series, and a guest curator for the Museum of American Finance. Formerly a clinical associate professor of economics at NYU's Stern School of Business, he is an expert in financial and political history and the author of half a dozen books on financial issues, most notably his recent work *One Nation Under Debt*, which was released in 2008.